CHAPTER ONE

Table of Contents and Introduction

Chapters and Appendices

The Goal of This Book

Beep... Beep.......…………... Beep... Beep

"Oh, this one has a good signal. Looks like it may be silver".

"What do you think it is dad?"

I smile because I am just as excited as my 9 year old son. We are about to uncover our next buried treasure... or not. The anticipation is half the fun.

"There is gold in them thar hills!".

Its also in local parks… at the beach… in yards… fields… the woods. Yes, pretty much everywhere.

Who wouldn't be hooked on the possibility of finding honest to goodness buried treasure? With metal detecting there is a good chance of that happening each time you go out. Well, it does depend on what your definition of treasure is!

There is something exciting about scanning an area of ground and hearing a very promising "beep" on your machine. What could it be? Maybe its a coin or two or more likely a pull tab from a can. But then again... maybe... it is something that can really get your heart fluttering.

Digging up any old coin is actually pretty exciting for many kids, even if its just a penny. When you find some gold however, that's when things get exciting. I am not necessarily talking about gold nuggets but gold jewelry. Nothing beats the thrill of poking through some dirt to see a very shiny gold and diamond ring staring back at you. The interesting thing about gold is that unlike most everything else you dig up, gold often looks as good as new even after years in the dirt or sand.

Unearthing every coin, buried relic or piece of jewelry immediately gets our imagination going. Who lost it here? When was the last time anyone has ever touched this? ... And yes: how much is it worth?

Metal detecting is so much more than finding valuables. It is the unearthing of history and rediscovering enticing clues as what went on at this very spot decades or even centuries ago. It is also about getting outdoors and enjoying your surrounding as well meeting some nice people along the way.

Welcome to the world of Metal Detecting (or MDing for short)!

It is one of the few hobbies that I know of that can actually pay for itself. You can't get into it thinking you are going to be striking it rich however. You need to balance your expectations a bit as we'll talk about shortly.

I am here to help you get off to a fantastic start into something which can very well end up being a life long hobby.

What This Book is About

This book is not intended to be the final word on all things metal detecting.

Instead, it is for people who are thinking about trying metal detecting or are the more beginning stages of their hobby. Maybe in the the first year or two of metal detecting. Someone who wants to get up to speed as quickly as possible. It is designed to give you the "need to know" information not just to get started but to move beyond the pure beginners stage.

It is information that I wish I had when I first started getting into metal detecting. It is written as if my friend had come to me asking for advice on getting the most out of their first couple of years of detecting.

While there is a lot of information available on metal detecting, some of it can be pretty technical in nature. Instead I'm focusing on some direct suggestions that are as practical as possible. This includes my recommendations on what machine to buy if you don't have one yet. If you already do have one, great! You will still learn a lot.

We will also look at what tools you may want to consider buying if you are really getting into the hobby.

You will learn the basics of everything you need to know to get started. Included are plenty of resources included for those who wish to dive deeper into the topic as well. There are also some great links to success stories to help fuel your enthusiasm even more.

While you'll learn a bit about how metal detectors work, we won't be going into the complexities of engineering that a more hard core metal detectorist may be looking for. No discussions of the circuitry set up of beat frequency oscillators to be found in here.

We will include some more technical discussions when appropriate however.

You will learn how to pick out good places to metal detect and also tactics that separate a good metal detectorists from those who struggle with it. You will be able to avoid making the most common mistakes that beginner metal detector hobbyists make when first get started.

There are some advanced tips sprinkled throughout the book as well for when you start getting serious about become an even better metal detectorist.

Let's get started!

Note About Links

For Your Convenience

I have included some relevant internet links in this book. I realize that being in a printed book, that may be a bit awkward but have no fear.

As a courtesy to you, I have compiled all of the links that are in here and I am happy to email them to you. You can then bring it up on your home computer and view them more conveniently there if you want.

There is no charge for that.

Just send me email at: tim@metaldetectortips.com with the subject line of: metal detecting links

I'll be happy to send you an email with all of the links in this book. You can then click on them when you are near your computer.

What Metal Detecting Is and Isn't

Its important to set your expectations about metal detecting.

It is a great way to spend more time outdoors in a hobby that literally anyone can do.

Spouses detect together.

Adults with their older parents can enjoy it.

It is easy enough that your kids or friends can tag along to help if you want as well. No real level of experience is needed to get a good taste of it. Of course when you decide you want to get even better at it, you can.

Bottom line, it is a great way to escape from it all for awhile and get some great alone time too. It can be a fantastic stress reliever to just head out, pop on your headphones and start finding buried "treasure".

What metal detecting is NOT is a get rich quick hobby. Many people starting out will find it challenging to get beyond a few modern coins in a local park unless they have the proper guidance. That's where this book comes in.

Yes you do have the potential for much more

interesting finds than a 2008 quarter by a swing set. That potential is greatly increased by applying tactics that only experience can provide. That experience can be your own (direct) experience or you can shorten the learning curve by learning from the experiences of others.

You may happen to be one of the lucky ones to find a hoard of gold, silver or ancient artifacts but don't be counting on it. It does happen on occasion but it is similar to winning the lottery... For some real life examples of those "winning the lottery" and finding some great things, see Appendix C at the end of this book for some success stories.

If you do want to do this with your young kids, it is important to realize it is not an activity that will typically hold your child's attention for hours at a time. That is unless you keep coming across find after find. Allow them to take a break, explore nature a bit and then call them over if you stumble across something particularly interesting.

My 9 year old son can tolerate about an hour and half at the beach on a slow day. If we are hitting find after find he is willing and able to stick with it longer. I am fine with that and can't blame him for getting a bit restless when it is slower going. Often he will find a good "walking stick" and whittle away on it (with safety in mind!) with his new found cub scout whittling skills. All the while keeping me company. He doesn't mind and I don't either.

My 7 year old daughter has a lower time tolerance and is usually good for 10 or 15 minute windows at a time. The majority of her time is exploring the area around me. If they are both joining me together, they are often checking out animals, bugs and just having an overall good time outside.

Either way, it beats them having their nose buried in a computer screen somewhere.

One last word of "warning".

The slow pace may not be for everyone.

Before you decide to start investing in tools and more equipment, I would recommend getting in a good 20 hours at the very minimum. That way you can have a sense if this is something you can see yourself sticking with. I wouldn't be surprised if it is, but it makes sense to hold off on extras a bit until you know you've been bitten by the detecting bug.

Benefits of Family Metal Detecting

As a parent of two kids (both just under 10 years old), one of the biggest benefits to me is that I get to spend excellent quality time with them. Outdoors. Away from a computer, t.v. or mobile device screen.

I've had multiple people comment on how nice it is to see my kids outside, truly enjoying nature for hours on end. The best part? My kids ask for it and prefer it to sitting around the house.

Not only are we outside getting fresh air, we are also getting good exercise. I've had many great conversations about nature and life in general while we were out MDing (metal detecting) together. When I am out on the beach, my 9 year old son is helping about 80% of the time and then exploring near me the other 20%. Your mileage may vary but I am happy just having that time together.

There is also an excellent social aspect to it.

When you are out on the beach, the people around you are usually quite curious as to what you may have found. It gives us many great opportunities to talk and joke with people. My favorite come back: "We are looking for land mines. We've found all but 2 of them. I know its around here somewhere".

Usually they laugh. If not, I tell them I'm kidding...

It is a great confidence and social skill builder for the kids. They quickly figure out that they have some knowledge that many adults don't have. More importantly people want to hear what they are more than willing to share about the hobby. You can tell they enjoy that attention quite a bit!

Now that we are into MDing more seriously, we are ramping up our research efforts as well. I include them in on that as much as they want to get involved. That includes how to research potential spots, how to secure permission to do it and finding out more about the things that we recover.

We've had discussions on private versus public property as well as respecting everyone's property.

Finally it is really getting them hooked on history. They were some what interested before but now it takes on a whole new meaning. You are recovering history from the ground. It is in your hand and up to you to perhaps figure out why it was there in the first place. If it wasn't for you, it would likely stay in the ground to rot or rust away over time.

I do a lot of activities with my kids including coaching baseball, fishing, golfing, etc, but metal detecting really comes out on top for all around quality time.

Tips for Introducing Kids to Metal Detecting

Here are some tips to help your kids get just as hooked as you are (or soon will be!).

Set Realistic Expectations

Its important to set expectations realistically. They are not going to be finding pirates gold on every adventure but honestly they are quite happy finding the lowly modern coin. That's great because there are PLENTY of those around.

I like to pre-hunt a spot before taking my kids there. If I am not sure how much potential a spot may have, I may hit it myself first for 1/2 an hour to get a feel for its potential. Obviously I have more patience than my kids so I try to stack the odds by advance scouting. I've gone to some new spots and quickly gotten multiple hits. I then will shoot home and grab my "assistant". I've also hit areas that were not productive and after a couple of hours, was glad I hadn't dragged one of my kids along to bore them to death!

Get Them Collecting

Kids love the idea of collecting things. There is no better thing to start collecting than the coins you are finding.

My son and I have an agreement. Any Wheat pennies we dig up are his to keep. "Wheaties" are older pennies minted from 1909 to 1956. They have a wheat design on the back of them. One of the first things I do when I dig up a penny is look at the back. I check to see if it is the Lincoln memorial or not. Those are newer pennies and affectionately known as a "Stinkin Lincoln". No offense to Lincoln. He just seems so much more handsome on the front of a wheat penny.

I bought a box of 20 pocket coin collecting pages. That ran about $6 and I bought them here: http://amzn.to/1pIzhSm

Any wheaties for a year he doesn't have yet goes into his collection. If we get a duplicate year then he decides which is the better example to keep on display.

His goal is to fill all of the years that wheaties were minted. He gets VERY excited when we turn up new ones. Especially if he doesn't have that year yet.

Often when I go out on my own, one of his first questions is "find any wheaties?".

This is a great tip for really getting your child hooked even more into the hobby.

Leave No Trace

Another good thing they are learning is how to do

their part in taking care of the environment. This also ties into helping to maintain the good reputation of metal detecting.

A big part of this is making sure that they properly fill in any holes that they dig. That applies to everywhere, including the beach. Nothing ruins people's perception of metal detecting faster than seeing various "gopher holes" that were left behind.

There is an art to digging out targets in the grass. By properly learning how to dig "plugs" or recover targets without even digging, then they will leave no trace behind that they were ever there. My kids know that is our goal each time, to make invisible holes. You will learn some techniques for that in an upcoming chapter.

Speaking of leave no trace, that includes trash that you've recovered. You will find PLENTY of beer tabs, bottle caps and crushed cans. I am a professional beer tab recovery expert. I never leave any of that behind. You dug it up, you own it until you can find the nearest trash barrel.

When we dig up something, we have a bag or a pouch just for that trash. Out on the beach we are not going around picking up after people but at the same time if we uncover a bottle cap or pull tab, it isn't right to toss it back in the hole and rebury it. Instead we do our part by removing that from the area.

You will be amazed at what you uncover in the sand. We have found everything from huge chunks of glass, nails, screws, open buck knives (pointing straight up under an inch of sand!) and even live bullets. If you are new to this, I guarantee you had no idea how much junk is lying just under the surface all around us.

Onlookers really appreciate the fact that we are not just out there "digging holes" but we are helping to make the area less free of trash.

The kids have learned to take pride in showing not only valuable items but also how much they have worked to help clean up the area. That is often just as impressive to people and it certainly leaves them with a positive impression of our hobby.

An Unexpected Benefit: Efficiency!

Once your "partner" (child, friend etc) becomes proficient at digging holes you can actually speed up your target locating. The secret is to bring golf tees.

When you get a good signal to dig, pinpoint it using your machine. Put a golf tee exactly above the target. My son and I use a code system of sorts. If I barely stick the tee in the ground, it means it is a shallow target.
Half way into the ground is for a medium 4 inch or so target while a tee nearly all the way down (but still visible in the grass) for deep 6"+ targets.

I use bright orange golf tees so they are the most visible.

The beauty of this is that you can go about finding multiple dig spots without having to slow down to actually dig. They can get to work on their new found plugging and popping skills to uncover the items. They will be armed with your handheld pinpointer (in our case our Garrett Pro Pointer). Once you get a half dozen or more spots marked, you can go and help yourself if you want. You can use your machine and trowel to help dig up some targets.

You will be amazed how much slowing down to dig interrupts your flow of finding targets. This tactic is a great way to maximize how many targets you can find. As a bonus, if you have to leave for the day, you can push the tees into the grass line to nearly hide them. If you know where to look you can find them when you return but they will not be sticking up too far. Golf tees are wooden as well so if by chance they did get hit by a lawn mower, it is not going to damage the mower at all. Just don't leave them there for an extended period of time. This is more of a "this spot is great and I am coming back in the morning" type of strategy.

This is fantastic for kids. They are truly being a big help and learning great pinpointing skills along the way.

Detecting With Friends

Travis and I recently connected with another metal detecting father / daughter duo. It is great when kids can meet other kids who are also into detecting with a parent. We have plans for some upcoming detecting together. Between helping out with the pinpointing and also just hanging out and being kids, it is some good quality time. Travis is looking forward to his next MD hunt with Anastasia already.

Memories

The time you spend with your kids MDing is likely to be remembered for a lifetime. When they get older they are likely to look back fondly as the great bonding time that they had with you.

You may also be responsible for them passing on this hobby to your grandkids someday. The great thing about this hobby is that it knows no age limits so you can be detecting with the grandkids as well!

Detecting For Seniors

Want to know a secret? Nearly all of the "seniors" that I talk to love the thought of trying metal detecting. They can join you! Even if they aren't actually swinging the machine, they can help you "pick out" the right spots or at the very least be there when you unearth each find. For those able bodied enough, it is easy to have them helping with a minute of instruction. Give them a hand held pinpointer detector and let them help you find the item in the hole once you've dug for it.

You would be surprised who would be interested in trying it. One detector friend I know worked very closely with a very wealthy high tech CEO. That man was worth just shy of a billion dollars when his company was bought out. He has a private plane, multiple houses and more money than he knows what to do with.

He also likes metal detecting. I guarantee he's not in it to get rich but instead for the thrill of the unexpected. What is about to be dug up?!?

Terminology Used in this Book

Let's take a quick look at some of the terms often used by metal detector hobbyists. Whether you're meeting one for the first time or discovering forums on the topic, it helps to know what some of these terms are. You can avoid sounding like a completely newbie by at least having some of the common phrases down.

Black Sand — Heavily mineralized soil that will often lead to false signals from your machine. Unfortunately its not uncommon for this to be near gold deposits. Just to make your life interesting!

Canslaw — A shredded aluminum can in the ground. Watch your fingers if you aren't using gloves!

Cellar hole — A deserted property where mostly all that exists are the stones of the foundation. These are often found in the woods and are often great places to look for old coins and artifacts. Be very careful on these types of property. They are often accompanied by very deep, abandoned wells. Sometimes these wells are hard to spot as they may have debris on them. You definitely want to avoid falling into that.

Coil — The round thing at the end of your detector that senses metal in the ground.

Coin Garden — The ability to plant pennies and nickels in order for them to grow up into dimes and quarters. Just kidding! A coin garden is a great way to test and practice with your equipment. Plant a variety of coins and metals in an out of the way location. Be sure to vary their depths from 1 to 8 inches or so. I use wooden golf tees to mark the location, item and depth of each item. For example, a quarter buried at 6 inches would have a golf tee directly above it with this notation: .25/6 - You can then practice on all of those items. Its important to note it may not be EXACTLY the same as all coins at those levels due to the halo effect (see below) but it is still worth doing.

Coin shooting — Focusing on just hunting coins. Someone coin shooting for the day may decide to ignore iron targets. They are focusing on coin signals and are not concerned about locating possible relic items.

Cache — An intentionally hidden collection of coins and/or jewelry. Everything from buried mason jars to Roman hordes of coins in clay pots. They are more common than most people would ever realize.

Coin spill — A find of several coins at once. Picture someone sitting on the grass and having the coins spill out of their pockets. Coin spills become interesting when you find ones that coins from a hundred years or more in them!

Dirt fishing — Metal detecting on soil – not on the beach.

Discrimination (or "Discriminating Out a Target") — The ability to set your machine to ignore certain types of signals. For example, in a particularly trashy area a machine can be set to ignore signals similar to pull tabs. Doing this is at the risk of not discovering some gold items however as they can sometimes appear to be in the same range. Some detectors have presets you can choose to automatically discriminate (eliminate) some signals if you are focusing on particular items. You need to think carefully before discriminating certain targets. Sure you found a few extra dimes but you missed that gold ring!

Find — Something found worth keeping. "Hey! Nice find!".

Halo Effect — Metal objects which have been in the ground for a while will start to emit ions around the object. Picture an old coin buried in the ground with a halo around it. It can help the coin be more detectable to your machine. As you dig or that earth is moved, the halo can disappear as it gets air. The effect is that a once strong signal can dissipate as you start digging. Some people swear this doesn't exist while many know it does. The halo effect is a reason why a freshly "planted" coin garden (see above) will not necessarily act the exact same as coins that have been buried for a long time.

High tone — A sort of squeal made by many multi-tone detectors when high conductivity targets (such as silver) are found. Typically desirable. "That's a nice high tone!"

Honey Hole — A digging spot which keeps producing

find after valuable find. Also known as "the spot who's location shall remain a closely guarded secret".

Low tone — An audible sound that typically represents low conductivity targets like iron, gold or or the dreaded pull tab.

Masking — When one less desirable target may be hiding a nearby desirable target. For example if you set your machine to ignore iron. If a coin is buried underneath a piece of iron, it may be masking the presence of it from your detector. A smaller coil often helps to differentiate between two closely placed objects in the ground. Higher end machines also handle this better in general.

MD - Metal Detector

Pinpointing — Using either a built in mode or a separate handheld "pinpointer" to determine a more precise location of a buried target. Many detectors have a built in pinpointing mode which helps you determine where to dig. Many MDers prefer to also have a handheld pinpointing device (such as a Garrett Pro Pointer, Minelab Profind etc).

Plug — A hole carefully dug in the ground so that dirt and grass are not harmed. Your goal when digging in grass every time is to dig a good plug. If no one can even tell that you have been there after the fact, then you've succeeded. This is probably THE biggest influence of the public's perception of our hobby so please (please) practice on leaving no trace behind.

This starts with digging a good plug.

Pull tab — Your nemesis. The kryptonite to your Superman abilities... Okay just exaggerating a bit. The can pull tab is something you will find plenty of. Who ever creates a more modern version that doesn't come off a can as easily deserves the Nobel Peace prize. When you are coin detecting, pull tabs often register in the same range as other potentially valuable items. In particular gold. You can discriminate them out so your detector ignores them but you are doing it at your own peril. You will also likely be ignoring some real finds now and then. It is a necessary evil to dig them up. Did I mention I don't like pull tabs?

Red Book — The annually published guide to coins and their values. Very informative to have and available at Amazon.com for under $20.

Relic hunters or iron diggers — A MD hobbyist who looks for items lost with more of a historical value besides coins. Searches often occur in fields, barns or woods. Examples are Civil War items such as bullets, belt buckles, buttons or anything else (not necessarily just for coins).

Sensitivity — Your detectors ability to get upset when you forget your anniversary of buying it. Actually it is a setting on your detector that allows you to make your detector less likely to produce false signals. Many machines perform best when not set to their highest sensitivity or else they become super sensitive. Just like an ex boy/girl friend, that can get annoying after awhile so dropping the sensitivity level down a bit helps to reduce false signals. You do this at the expense of loss of some depth however. If you are getting a lot of false signals then it is usually worth it however to save your sanity.

Target — A buried, unknown object that is detected by your metal detector.

Target ID (TID) — Many machines have the ability to give you some indication of what it thinks it senses in the ground. On some models it can be a graph of sorts with a light up notch under a pull tab or .25 icon. The deeper a target is in the ground, the less accurate the TID is likely to be. A TID is also often an audio tone as well. A low tone generally indicates something like iron while a higher audio tone may be silver.

Tot Lot — Where single dads go to meet single moms. Also where many coin shooters (see definition above) go to find clad (see definition above). These are children's playgrounds with many opportunities for coins to be lost under benches, slides, swing sets…. Pretty much anywhere. They are a good starting point for a lot of new MDers to get practice and to fill their piggy banks.

VDI — A numerical indication on some detectors indicating the possible identity of an object. Machines can vary as to what their VDI corresponds to. It is one reason to get some good quality time in with your machine. It can help to Google your machine's model and: VDI - You may find other people's lists of VDI numbers which can tell you "a VDI 18 on x machine = a nickel. A VDI of 80 = a dime" etc. Again, it will vary based on what you are using but it is definitely good to know.

Terminology Part 2: Coins

As you get into the hobby, you will hopefully end up checking out forums and videos related to metal detecting. At first it may seem like the people are talking in a foreign language. They use some slang or lingo for various types of coins so you may see a post something like this:

"Just returned from a great dig. Found my second SLQ for the year, a seated, a couple Barbers and (yes finally!) a draped bust! Next to a Reale or a tree shilling, this was on my bucket list. A few toasted coppers were there which I am still trying to date."
If some (or most) of that made little sense, fear not. Here are the most common slang coins that you are likely to come across. There is a caveat to this as it is U.S. coins primarily. I will be VERY happy to include other regions of the world if anyone wants to contribute input on those. I will update the book if I do get suggestions on frequently mentioned coins to add. I can be reached at tim@metaldetectortips.com

Barber coin — U.S. Dimes, quarters and half dollars minted from 1892 until 1916. They are 90% silver and desirable to collectors.

Buffalo Nickel — Minted between 1913 and 1938, this 5 cent piece is 75% copper and 25% nickel. The 1913 type I Buffalo's are rare and very collectible.

Clad — New coins which have been created with mostly non-precious metals – this are typically silver-colored U.S. coins minted after 1964. This term also applies to pennies minted after 1958. These are indicative of more recent activity by people. A location that has little clad, but more older coins is very desirable. It is likely less picked over by metal detector hobbyists so far.

Draped bust – An American coin minted from 1795 to 1808. A very desirable find.

Indian Head Penny (IH) — A U.S. penny minted from 1859 to 1909. It is 88% copper. Certain years and mint marks are desirable to coin collectors. Plus they are just plain cool looking in my opinion. Finding IH pennies is usually a good sign there is probably some old silver coins in the area as well.

Large Cent — A U.S. coin worth 1/100th of a dollar. They were minted from 1793 to 1857 and replaced by the much smaller penny. There were style variations of large cents including "capped" which had Lady Liberty with a cap on her hair. "Braided" large cents had Lady Liberty with braided hair.

Memorials — A US one cent coin with the Lincoln memorial on one side (1959 to present). Sometimes affectionately referred to as a "stinkin' Lincoln". No offense meant towards Lincoln but he drew the short straw when he was assigned to the lowly penny!

Merc or Mercury — A US Mercury Dime minted from 1916-1945. Although it is a depiction of a young lady Liberty with a winged cap, it is commonly mistaken as being the Roman God Mercury. Either way, its a dime with a woman's head with wings attached. Desirable as it is 90% silver.

Morgan — The Morgan Silver Dollar minted from 1878-1921. Desirable as it is 90% silver.

Rosie — A 90% silver Roosevelt dime. Minted from 1946-1964.

Seated — A US coin minted from 1837 - 1891 in half dime, dime, quarter and half dollar. Desirable.

Spanish Real (pronounced Ree-Al) — Silver coins in 1/2, 1, 2, 4 and 8 reales denominations. The 8 Reales was known as the Spanish dollar or "piece of eight" from pirate lore. These were a common currency used in the U.S. before the colonies were settled and started minting their own money. Much like the U.S. dollar is a worldwide currency now, Spanish Reales were similarly used worldwide into the 1800's.

Standing Liberty Quarter ("SLQ") — A U.S. coined minted from 1916 to 1930. It took the place of the Barber quarter. Desirable to collectors and it is 90% silver.

Trime — A U.S. 3 cent coin minted from 1851 to 1889.

Wheatie — US penny with wheat stalks on the back

of it. Minted from 1909-1958.

While we are talking about old coins, here is an interesting link I came across. It lists the top 50 U.S. coins of all times. Specific years and mint marks for different types. Its worth comparing some of your older coins to this list. You may have a valuable year or mint on one without even knowing it:

http://www.pcgs.com/News/The-Top-50-Us-Coins-Of-All-Time

How to Contact Us

As mentioned you can get an email with a list of links mentioned through out this book. Just send an email with the subject link "Metal Detector Links". You can reach us at tim@metaldetectortips.com

We are also VERY receptive to feedback, suggestions or additions to add to this book.

Travis and I would love to hear from you! Give us a bit of background as to whether you are just starting or not, which machine you have (or are considering) and generally where in the world you are located.

CHAPTER TWO

Detector Basics: Equipment

Types of Detector Technology

First a warning. I am about to go slightly tech geeky on you. I just wanted to explain the most common types of detectors. You will inevitably see references to this as you explore the hobby. This will at least give you the "need to know" basics on it.

There are a few different ways that detectors do what they do.

One of the earliest was called BFO (Beat Frequency Oscillator). It is no longer in use but it was one of the earliest methods of sending and receiving signals into the ground and back.

More common these days are two different options.

PI - Pulse Induction

These are not the machine of choice for trashy areas or places where you wish to discriminate out iron. To discriminate means to set your detector not to alert when that senses a particular type of metal. Again PI is not the type of machine for that type of environment.

However for relic and deep hunting, PI machines are very desirable.

PI machines are also the preferred machine for most serious gold nugget hunters. They search deeper for large nuggets and are good for mineralized ground. Gold is typically found in ground with a lot of minerals and the PI handles it well. A downside is that they are not particular good at finding smaller items, like flecks of gold. Nuggets? Great. Flecks, just so so on older machines. Anecdotal stories indicate that newer PI machines however are becoming much better at smaller nuggets as well. Expect to pay top dollar initially for those benefits.

It has pluses and minuses.

VLF - Very Low Frequency

This is more of the "jack of all trades" technology. They are good choice for entry level and "pro-sumer" machines. Pro-sumer being for customers who are also somewhat professional in the hobby as well.

A majority of detectors on the market use VLF technology and it can handle just about any situation you throw at it. It may not be the best at say, finding gold, but it can certainly do that. There are some VLF machines that are more specialized in gold detecting and they have more than enough success stories to prove they do work.

My recommendation for most people is to start off with a good VLF machine. The entry level Ace 250 is a good, viable VLF machine as is the Fisher Fs. There are plenty of other ones as well.

Some worthy VLF, gold focus machines include these in no particular order:
Minelab Eureka Gold, Fisher Gold Bug II, White's GMT, Garrett AT Gold, Fisher Gold Bug Pro, and Tesoro Lobo SuperTRAQ.

The reality is that most serious gold hunters have both a PI and a VLF machine.

Next we will look at specific recommendations if you don't have a machine yet.

Choosing A Detector

The biggest question someone starting out in metal detecting has is "which metal detector should I buy"? Ask a hundred experts and you are likely to get dozens of answers, especially when it comes to the more expensive machines.

If you haven't bought a machine yet and are still making up your mind, pay attention here.

There are plenty of makers of metal detectors to choose from: Minelab, Garret, Fisher, E-Trac, Technetics. Tesoro, Whites... Those are just a few of many. Then to further confuse things, they offer various models so literally you are talking dozens of different possibilities.

Some are quite good.
Some are quite expensive.
Some are just 'okay'.

They can vary in what they can be used for as well. Some are for hunting primarily gold nuggets.

Others are for underwater.

Some are all purpose which are pretty good across the board.

This is where the confusion for a new buyer comes in.

A far majority of people getting into detecting fit into a certain profile.

They are looking for a good "all round" machine that is affordable and can detect nearly anything that is out there. Gold, coins, silver, jewelry and relics (think civil war artifacts).

If you fit into that profile, then I have good news. I do have a specific recommendation. Now like many times in life, everyone has their own opinion and I am not trying to start a brand war here. If you already have a different model than I am going to recommend, and you are happy with it, then that is excellent.

This is not a dig (pun intended) on your own personal favorite entry level machine.

I just know that this machine has made a lot of people happy and worked well enough to keep them hooked on the hobby. It quite often has paid for itself (and more) with its finds.

So if a friend says "I want a good, all around detector that is easy to learn and won't break the bank" then I recommend the Garrett Ace 250.

This a very affordable machine (just over $200) that has many features of machines costing 3x as much. It has become THE top selling machine for people getting started in MDing. Don't be fooled by its price tag though. It is extremely capable and is used quite successfully by many people.

My philosophy is simple. The Ace 250 will let you get experience in metal detecting with a minimum investment (right around $200). If you decide that its not for you, the typical used Ace 250 can be resold for between $150 and $175.

On the other hand buying a new $1,000 machine has more of a risk. Typically a used machine in that price range would go for about $750 or $800. Even if it only had 3 hours of use on it.

Very recently I saw someone on a forum announce they got a $1495 machine that everyone was talking about. Well, it turned out he didn't like it as much as he anticipated. That machine was being sold by him on Craigslist for a $300 loss you a few weeks later.

There are people that started with a Garrett Ace and eventually do buy a higher end machine once they are hooked on the hobby. The reality is though, many of them still hang on to their Ace because it is still a capable machine. It is also lighter than many other models and they have grown affection for it.

Often they keep it as a back up machine. They also have it as a loaner for a friend. It could even be lent to a friendly property owner who just gave you permission to detect on their property.

Believe or not, many MD hobbyists really look at their

machine(s) as have a personality of sorts.

Some are very good under certain condition while lacking a bit in other conditions. The Garrett Ace 250 is a great all around choice and it is rare to have a model nearly as widely recognized as a very capable machine.

I know you are my friend now (after all you got this book!) but you don't have take my word for it. Google this:
Garrett Ace 250 review

Review after review after review are singing its praises. Plenty of Youtube videos on it as well if you search for that phrase on Youtube.com

This is not to say there aren't other capable machines in the $200 - $350 price range. There are and you may be just happy (or more so) if that is what you start off on. The Fisher F2 for example is a capable starter model which many people are happy with. If I hadn't started with the Ace, I would have went for the Fisher F2. Some prefer it over the Ace 250.

Its just my personal opinion (and that of many other people) that you wouldn't regret getting the Ace 250 as the first machine to start off with. Like I said, if you don't like it, post it on Craigslist and you will have most of your money back very quickly.

I purchased mine through Kellyco for $202.45. The link I used at that time was this one:

http://www.kellycodetectors.com/garrett/garrett-ace250.htm

The price at the time was $212.45 but they offered a bundle. They included headphones (which are not always included) as well as a knife, pouch, magnifying glass and some other odds and ends. It included free shipping.

Money Saving Tip:: During the checkout process, I noticed there was a box for "promotion code". To me that always means the opportunity to save more money.

On Google.com I searched for: kellyco promotion code

I found a site which had a valid "$10 off your order" from Kellyco. I put that code into the shopping cart page and sure enough, my order came to $202.45. I was very happy with that price considering it included headphones (which although may be cheap, they are a start!).

See that? You just paid for the price of this book with one tip.

You're welcome!

My order arrived within a few days and I was happy with the process.

I was thrilled by the machine.

Keep in mind this was a recommendation for a good general purpose machine.

It is not 100% waterproof. The coil and all the way up to the control box is waterproof. The control box however is NOT waterproof.

You could search a bit in the water if you were very careful about not getting the control box wet, but you are taking that chance.

A good waterproof model is the Garrett AT Pro. It costs more than the 250 but it is more of a "pro-sumer" model detector. That is professionals as well as the average consumer can use it. You can literally swim with it underwater if you have the optional underwater head phones which they have available.

Okay, I hear you saying: "...but I want to find gold as well!".

You can find gold with these models. They are just not as specialized as a true gold metal detector.

The issue with gold prospecting is that the ground that gold is found in is often mineralized. That means a lot of potential false signals for a detector which is not specifically designed for gold. The trade off of getting

45

a gold detector (besides the high price tag) is they are not as good (generally) at coin and relic hunting. That is intentional. Gold detectors are focused on that one goal of finding gold.

As you get into the hobby, you are going to feel the urge to go to higher end machines. They detect objects more deeply and accurately. They also specialize in certain conditions. Examples of some exceptional mid to higher end machines include Minelab's E-trac, CTX 3030 as well as another brand XP Deus (pronounced Day-us). There are others to so don't get offended if I didn't mention your favorite make or model.

Don't jump right into a $1500 - $2500 machine first thing. Get started with an intro machine and go from there.

Detector Accessories

Hand Held Digging Tools

Metal detecting is all about digging. Whether it is in loose sand, wet sand or dirt... having the right tool for the job will make things go much more quickly and enjoyably.

Generally there are three types of digging to think about. Beach, dirt and other.

Since most people in the world don't leave near a beach, let's start with non-beach digging.

Arguably the best digging tool for cutting into grass or dirt is a Lesche digging tool.

I ordered my Lesche through Amazon.com here, where it has 5 out of 5 stars (which is extremely rare): http://amzn.to/1qDCVRj

It isn't cheap at just under $37 but it is built like a tank.

The Lesche has a solid steel, double edged 7 inch blade, serrated on one edge with great root cutting teeth. It feels like I am wielding a short sword when I have it out. In a pinch it would probably do pretty good defending me against some brush monster attacking me.

It cuts plugs very easily and is quite handy sawing through in ground debris when needed.

It is likely to be the only digging trowel tool you will ever have to buy. That is assuming you don't lose it. Then again if you do lose it in the grass, at least you have a metal detector to find it!

Cheaper digging tools can be had at any gardening or hardware store but the issue is... you get what you pay for.

Here is an under $20 choice that I like as well. It is the one I bought for my son which cost $16.49 at the time. It can be found here: http://amzn.to/1mqF558

Don't expect a $10 or $15 trowel or digging tool to last forever. Particularly if you have hard or rocky ground in the areas you want to metal detect. They may last for a bit before bending or breaking.

The Lesche tool mentioned above is not going to do that.

They come in left or right handed versions. The left handed has a serrated blade on the left vs. the right handed on the other side. Even though I am a righty, I chose the left handed version. I like to stick the tool into the ground and then "cut" the soil in a clockwise direction. It is just a matter of preference and either will work.

Here is my trusty Lesche and the included belt holster for it.

Shovels

As good as a hand held trowel can be, sometimes it is desirable to have something larger like a shovel. Relic hunting or detecting in the woods are good times to have a good digging shovel.

I personally have a (Lesche) Sampson T-Handle 31 inch shovel.

I purchased it here:
http://amzn.to/1qc1S4g

It is built as rock solid as the Lesche hand tool. It has a large blade and also can be used while standing up.

A slightly more expensive option is the Predator tool which is also an exceptional digging tool. Interestingly enough, this is also built by Lesche but under a different company name. There was a messy divorce involved at some point and the Lesche family split. The Predator is made by the Lesche founder while the handheld Lesche are made by the (former) family business. That sounds messier than metal detecting in a pig pen.

Anyways... here is where you can see and order the Predator if you are interested:

http://predatortools.com/

Until you are committed to this hobby, you can get by with a spade shovel from a local hardware store. They won't be as efficient or sturdy but can get you by in the meantime.

If you are just getting started and/or on a budget, you can get by with a small spade shovel available at most hardware stores. They have very limited ability to cut through roots however and are also not as sturdy as the other shovels I just mentioned..

Probing Tools

Along the lines of digging tools are also probing tools. It will help you poke in and pry out a target that you are hitting on. A simple flat head screw driver is usually sufficient for this but you may want to make one modification so that you don't scratch coins you are probing.

I dipped the very end of mine in "Plasti-Dip". This is a liquid rubber coating that drys to form a tough rubber/plastic layer on the tool. I got a jar of it for under $8 at Home Depot so you may want to check with hardware stores local to you. You can always peel off the coating anytime you want to return the tool back to normal. Then you can re-coat it again if you wish.

Some people prefer to sand or grind down the end of a long screwdriver to blunt the point.

Another option is to use the broken tip from an old fishing pole. Use the fiber glass rod as a make sure probe. That likely won't damage any coins you may poke with it.

Sand Sifting Tools

For digging at the beach, a sand sifter is very desirable to have. They come in all shapes and sizes. Some are hand sifters and others have a handle. Hand sifters require a lot of bending over. That is not necessarily a bad thing for kids as they are more manageable for them to handle. For an adult however, we have further to bend over and well, frankly it can get a bit tiring kneeling down, scooping, searching, scooping, standing up to scan, bending over again... you get the point.

A decent pole sifter can run anywhere from around $50 for a PVC plastic model (search ebay) to stainless steel high end models running $150 to $200.

If you do get an all metal one, consider getting stainless steel if you want to avoid rust and corrosion.

In our team, Travis prefers to sift, pinpoint and recover the finds while I work the detector itself. Although the machine is light (2.7 lbs) it still becomes heavy due to his size.

Miscellaneous Equipment

A detector sling (Detector Buddy or Slingy Thingy)

A few hours of swinging a metal detector back and forth can get a bit tiring. I have one of the lightest models there is (Garrett Ace 250 at 2.7 pounds) but even that can get a bit tiresome on my right arm. Slingy Thingy to the rescue.

A good detector sling helps support the detector and is extremely easy to use. It removes your arm from having to maintain the "lift" portion of the work involved. Instead a detector sling does the work and you can basically maintain the swinging motion with just a finger or two.

I have the "Detecting Buddy" which I got on sale for $19.95 here:
http://www.extremedetecting.com/DetectingBuddy.html

The competitor to that is the Swingy Thingy which is twice as much. I prefer the simplicity (and price!) of the Detecting Buddy myself but you can check out the Swingy Thingy at:
www.swingythingy.com

Pinpointing Tools

Many detectors come with a built in pinpointer type option.

You would locate the general area of your target. Make a visual mental note of the spot where the target is. Then move your detector away from that so it is not picking up metal. Then switch to pinpointing mode.

In the case of the Garrett there is a pinpoint button you hold down. You then slowly criss cross over the target area. Go left/right and then up/down over it. The loudest tone and highest reading is when the stem in the middle of your coils is directly over the target.

To get even more pinpoint accuracy as to where it is, take a look at this youtube video. It describes how to pinpoint exactly where a target is buried. http://www.garrett.com/hobbysite/hbby_at_pro_dd_pinpointing.aspx

That video shows a Garrett detector but other machines may act similarly. If you have a different model then search for that on YouTube. There are bound to be some examples.

Only experience, trial and error will help you become proficient at this but it is worthwhile skill to acquire. Not only will digs be faster due to your accuracy but you will also end up digging up smaller holes.

As good as the built in pinpointing tool may be, a handheld pinpointer is even better. So much so that I dedicated the next chapter to just that.

Does Size Matter? Coil Sizes

The coil is the business end of your metal detector. That is where the electronic pulses are being sent into the ground to be interpreted as they bounce back up.

All detectors come with an initial coil size but many of them let you change the size of the coil if you wish.

Using the Garrett Ace 250 as an example, it comes stock with a 6.5 x 9 inch, elliptical shaped coil.

This size is a great, all purpose coil size. It is capable of detecting coins, gold, silver and pretty much everything else. It may not be the BEST at locating those but it does a good job in general and is a good starting choice size.

As a general rule, the depth that a coil can detect a coin sized object is roughly equal to its diameter. So in the case of the stock 6x9 coil then that is what you may experience for depth at a strong sensitivity. Approximately 6 to 9 inches deep. A larger object has the potential for even deeper. Even coins could be sensed deeper as ground conditions also factor into the performance. Again, that is a general rule of thumb but something to keep in mind.

Okay, then why would you need a bigger or smaller coil?

Different sizes excel (or not) in different situations. Let's take a look at each.

Smaller Coils

One example of a smaller coil is the 4.5 inch "Sniper" coil. It has the circumference of about a softball. As the name alludes, it has more pinpoint accuracy.

PROS: Smaller coils are good for really trashy areas. If you are in an environment with a lot of pull tabs or iron junk, a smaller coil let's you "see" (sense) each target more individually underground. So a pull tab an inch or two away from a coin is more likely to give you separate signals. A larger coil generally does not have that level of finesse in discriminating except on higher end machines.

Another positive aspect is because the coil is physically smaller, it can get in hard to reach places. Out in the woods particularly. I know I have tangled with some roots or bushes with a larger coil in the past. A smaller one may have made much easier work of sniffing out the tight spots. I can only imagine if I was running a really large coil out there. It would not be fun trying to navigate that around in the brush.

Smaller coils are also better at detecting around metal objects like bleachers. Because the signals are so concentrated in such a small area, it is tends to lead to less interference than a large coil would produce in that same circumstance.

CONS: You are likely giving up search depth. Using the rule of thumb you can expect a 4.5" depth but many users swear they don't notice any significant difference between a small coil and the standard coil.

Another draw back is the less area it is covering. You have to do 1.5 to 2 times as many swings with a 4.5 coil to cover the same area that a 6x9 coil would cover. It would need nearly 3 swings to cover what a 9x12 inch coil could cover in one.

Just to give you an idea of cost, smaller coils (at least for Garrett) run about $70 on Amazon. Here is the cheapest I could find: http://amzn.to/1iEj9NB

Larger Coils

On the larger side of things some coils can be quite huge. I've seen them up to 18 x 15 inch but there are likely bigger ones as well. A more common large size example would be a 9 x 12.

PROS: The biggest benefit of large coils is additional depth. If you really want to search deep, then these can help out. They are most suitable for someone who is hunting larger items like relics or caches of items.

CONS: Bigger coils are more bulky and tend to

weight more. The larger ones can also sometimes suffer from not having the pinpoint accuracy that a smaller coil would have. They throw a large beam out but it is not as concentrated as a small coil. This is particularly true of coils that are 15 inches or more. A coin size shape buried deep may be more challenging.

Large coils generally run from just under $100 to several hundred depending on the make and model.

Coil Covers

While we are on the subject of coils, a coil cover is a great investment. It is a plastic cover that goes underneath the coil and fits it like a glove. It does not alter the performance of the detector at all and often you can not even tell it is in place without looking closely. Coils can and do get damaged. It is inevitable that you are going to swing into a rock or scrape it across something abrasive.

COST: For under $20, a coil cover is well worth it. Here is the one that I purchased for my stock Ace 250 coil: http://amzn.to/1kuA2i7

By now you may be having the "3 bears syndrome". This coil is too large (and heavy). This coil is too small (and doesn't cover enough area). Some people settle for the "aaaahh.. This coil is just about right for most things". This is where the mid size range of coils comes into play.

This is the reason that my starting detector of choice (the Garrett Ace 250) comes with a 6.5" x 9" inch coil. It is a nice middle ground between being too big and heavy, versus too small.

That isn't to say that I don't own other coils, because I do. Mostly I keep the standard one on however and put on the sniper coil for parks that have a lot of pull tabs. If I am relic hunting and/or covering a huge field, then a larger coil is usually my top choice.

If I HAD to only use one, I would pick my stock coil due to its good overall general capabilities. The detector manufacturers intentionally have their models come with a good all around coil to appeal to as many people as possible for general conditions.

Bottom line advice to my friend would be: wait until you have many dozens of hours of detecting time out of the way. You will have a much better sense of what coil you may want to invest in (if any). In the meantime, your stock coil is likely to still do well for you.

Proper Coil Movement

As simple as it may seem, there is a correct and many incorrect ways to swing your detector's coil above the ground.

It is important to do it correctly to ensure that your machine is as accurate as possible. This will help you locate as many of the goodies beneath your feet as possible. Incorrect movement of the coil can also frustrate you with added false signals as well as loss of depth.

The coil should be just above the surface you are scanning. An inch or less is perfect. Not much higher than that, as much as you can help it. Every inch you come up from the ground is an inch you lost in depth.

You want to avoid banging your coil against any rocks or hard ground. They can and will break with enough abuse.

Its important that your coil stays the same height off the ground during your entire swing back and forth. The rookie mistake is to swing up the coil at the end of each pass. This incorrect swing looks like a pendulum swinging.

This will result in false signals as well as lost target opportunities. Keep the coil at a consistent distance from the ground the whole time as shown here:

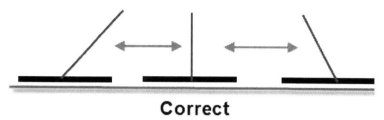

Correct

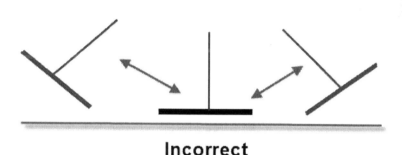

Incorrect

When discovering a promising target in the ground, slowly wave the coil in a Left / Right pattern. The coil is slowly moved in sweeps from side to side. I prefer my sweeps to take about 2 full seconds or more. If you go too fast you will miss signals, especially deep ones. A very fast sweep will often pick up something near the very top of the surface but you will miss many smaller or deeper targets. Again, slow down for deeper signals. That last point is a REALLY important one so if you skimmed right over without fully soaking it in, give a reread.

One blogger I follow is an absolute maniac with finding silver coins. His best year was over 1,100 and usually averages over 500 silver coins a year.

When asked about his swing speed, he says that if he can see it moving, then its too fast. He was only half joking but he does swing VERY slowly because he is going after deeply buried silver coins. Keeping this tip in mind will quickly make a difference for you to excel at MDing.

Watch the coil head to see when it is alerting.

During this time, I am also paying attention to the control panel read out to see what is registering on there. If it is alerting consistently, along with a strong indication of a coin finding, this is a hopeful sign.

TIP: To make it easier for me visually, I have marked a point on my detector coil with a bit of yellow tape. It is a good reference point for me to refer to when pinpointing the exact location of a buried target. It helps my son to visualize it a bit better as well with that yellow tape.

The side to side sweeps are illustrated with the arrows below. This is done until you get a good visual idea of where it keeps alerting.

First narrow down side to the target lies in the gi

With experience you will get very good about making a mental picture in your head of where it is on the ground.

Now move 90 degrees "to the side" of the target. Your swings that were covering it say, from east/west, are now covering it from north/south as illustrated here:

Next scan the other

After several slow passes you should now have a very good mental image of where your target is.

Be sure you notice how deep it is registering and also what it is showing up as on your machine.

At this point, I like to take a guess as to what it is based on what the machine is telling you.

I play this mental game with every target hit. This is an excellent way to start honing in your detecting skills. Initially you may not be too accurate but over time you are going to start recognizing patterns with your machine. This can help reinforce how well you are becoming adept with it.

Now that you have a good approximate idea of where the target is, you can narrow it down even more by putting the coil directly over the area. Then use the technique shown here:

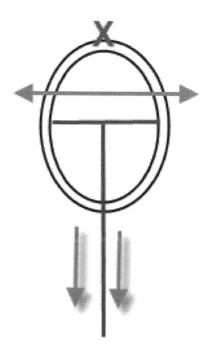

Move your coil slight
side to side while
pulling towards you
When the signal fade
the target is just in
front of the coil.

That may vary from machine to machine.If this seems a bit confusing, it won't soon enough.

Weak Signals

A target in the ground can present a weak signal to you for a variety of reasons.

It may be deep or a small target.

It could also be a coin that is laying vertically in the ground instead of horizontally.

If you are picking up a weak signal, its a good tactic to change positions. So if the target is in front of you, move slightly to its side and then swing the coil over that same area. It is not uncommon for the signal to now be stronger from that angle.

Using Your Machines Built In pinpointer

If your machine has a pinpoint feature built in, it can also greatly help locate the target very quickly.

As an example, on the Ace 250, there is a pinpoint button. Press the button while it is slightly away from the target. Then move it to where you suspect the target is.

Watch the bar indicator on the control panel. It will get

higher or lower based on how close you are to being directly over the buried item. When it is at full bars, then the stem of your machine is directly over at least part of the object. You should then use this feature to see how big the object is. If the indicator is showing full bars and the object is 6 inches+ long, it is not likely one coin. It could be a can or big piece of metal. If it is a coin sized area then it is a good indication that the object may be coin or pull tab in size. If it is REALLY small in size when pinpointing, it may be a b.b. sized object or perhaps a small stud earring.

Again with practice you will get very good at determining ahead of time what the object is likely to be. Soon you will be able to visualize what the shape and size is pretty accurately. Even to the point of knowing if something is round and hollow (like a ring) or very small.

Whenever you use your machine's pinpointer make sure you are paying attention to where the actual item is discovered. You can learn to get VERY precise with it as you built up practice but ONLY if you are checking your results. This is one instance where practice does make perfect (or nearly perfect!). It is a handy built in tool to have if your machine does have it.

What Many New Detectorists Don't Realize

Many machines are calibrated to alert the strongest to coin shaped objects. So a round, metallic object the size of a quarter is going to look really enticing to a detector. That doesn't mean it IS a coin as there are plenty of other metal objects of that shape (especially bottle caps!). The machine is making its best guess estimate if the object is a possible coin.

Sometimes if something is big, round but very deep it could confuse the machine. What may look like quarter size could be a round piece of metal the size of a dinner plate 18 inches down.

Remember there is only one way to know with 100% accuracy what is being detected. That is by digging it up!

An experienced detectorist can likely make a good guess as to what an object is but you never know for sure until you dig. Ignore decent targets at your own risk. It could be a very valuable coin or piece of jewelry.

Practicing Ahead of Time

I live in New Hampshire. My kids were anxious to try some metal detecting. Unfortunately there was still snow on the frozen solid ground. This did not make for ideal metal detecting conditions. The thought of digging in frozen ground… in the cold… for a coin… didn't strike me as a good introduction to detecting for them.

I figured out a way to get them some practice before the snow melted off the ground.

In our house we have several area rugs. When the kids were not in the room, I hid various items under different parts of the rug. A large towel or even a blanket could be used as well.

I hid quarters, dimes, nickels, pennies, a gold ring, a nail, some gum wrapper foil and an aluminum bottle cap.

They then came in the room and used the detector to locate each target. They got used to the sound and read out for each type of target. I had them pay attention to the tone as to whether it was high or low.

A very low tone would often be for "junkier" type metal such as iron or foil. The higher pitched tones were for certain types of coins. The detector we use has a distinctive "ca-ching" slot machine type sound for coins such as quarters and half dollars.

They not only used the machine to pinpoint and identify the target before I revealed what it was, but they also used the pinpoint feature on the detector to locate more precisely where it was. By holding down the pinpoint button, you then wave the coil over the target. The loudest and strongest signal is when the stem of the machine is directly over the target.

They made a visual note of where that was. This let them get used to using our handheld pinpointing tool to find out EXACTLY where it was under the rug. We have a Garrett Pro Pointer for this. It not only sounds but vibrates when it detects metal. The faster it sounds, the closer it is. When it is touching or nearly touching the target then it is a solid tone.

The kids enjoyed playing this game and it was practical. They were easily able to train their ears for what type of item was being detected. This becomes important out in the field to help them readily identify different targets.

Now keep in mind this won't imitate the exact conditions of coins underground most of the time. It does give them a general idea however. More importantly gets them a bit of fun MD time.

You may find your house has too much electrical interference to do this indoors. You may also be detecting nails and wires under the floor. In that case you could put items a bit higher up. Take a long empty box and tape the coins inside the box in spots so they can't see it. It should be high enough to help prevent false signals. Turning down your sensitivity may help with this excercise as well.

Practicing Part 2 - Coin Gardens

A coin garden is what the name implies. A spot in your yard where you bury coins and other metallic objects. This gives you an area to test actual buried targets.

Here's one way to do it.

Get a collection of the 3 each of the following:

Quarters, dimes, nickels, pennies, bottle caps, pull tabs, nails and if you happen to have some older silver coins, a few of them too.

Somewhere in the corner of your yard, bury one type of each item about 1 inch down. You don't even have to dig, just push is it into the dirt so it is not visible. Each item should be at least a couple feet a part if you have the space. Then you can practice your plug digging. Plant another row of items a couple feet away. This time put the items in about 5 inches down.

Finally a 3rd row about 7 or 8 inches down.

You may want to mark the corners of the area and then note which items you have. It can be simple such as this:

All items are 2 feet apart. Each row is 2 feet apart:

Row 1" deep .25 — .10 — .05 — .01 — BC —
PT — Nail — Silver
Row 4" deep .25 — .10 — .05 — .01 — BC —
PT — Nail — Silver
Row 7" deep .25 — .10 — .05 — .01 — BC —
PT — Nail — Silver

BC = bottle cap
PT = pull tab

If you want you can mark the location of items with golf tees. Use a sharpie permanent marker and write on the side what the object buried underneath is. That isn't a bad way to start but I would remove them after a bit of practice so you aren't cheating anymore by going straight to each tee.

This is a great practice field to see how your detector reactors to various objects at various depths. You can also mix up the rows a bit if you want so they are not the same items in the same order.

But wait, here's an important point. When you first bury a coin it is not the exact same conditions compared to a coin that has been buried for weeks, months or years.

There is a much disputed term called a "halo effect" with buried metal. I am convinced it is legitimate as are many other detectorists. If you are not then don't take offense.

The halo effect is based on the theory that most metal (except pure gold) ionizes in the ground over time. This ionization gets trapped around the coin by the surrounding soil. The effect of this is that it is much more readily sensed by metal detectors because it is creating a larger target for it.

You may find that your detector has a hard time locating a deeper coin that you just planted. That same coin with a halo effect will make it stand out more.

So like a fine wine, your coin garden will get better with time. Well, it will at least be a more accurate representation of what your detector may or may not report under similar circumstances out in the field.

By the way most gold you will find detecting is not pure gold. It is 10k, 14k, 18k etc. These are a combination of gold and some other alloy to help make the jewelry stronger. Pure gold is 24K but is softer and more likely to scratch so it is not generally something you are going to find in day to day jewelry too often. Its the other alloys that are mixed in with the gold that will be creating the halo effect if there is one.

Geek Alert: For a technical discussion of this halo effect you can check out this article:
http://www.njminerals.org/metaldetecting-haloeffect.html

Metal Detecting Etiquette

Metal Detecting enthusiasts that have their own brotherhood/sisterhood of sorts. If you are metal detecting, you are now part of that group so welcome aboard!
Along with the free "membership" comes responsibility. In particular some etiquette do's and don'ts. There are various version of this code of ethics but they all say about the same thing. Raise your right hand and repeat after me:

* I will never trespass or dig without permission.

* I will not harm or alter an property, even if it appears abandoned.

* I will leave gates open or closed as I found them.

* I will remove all trash that I dig up and properly dispose of it.

* I will use proper digging techniques and fill in all of my holes, regardless of where I dig them. My goal is to leave no trace behind.

* I will report any historically significant find to the local historical society, park rangers or other authorities which may be specified by law.

* I will not dig in a site which has been labeled as archaeologically significant.

* I will obey all laws and ordinances regarding metal detecting and the area to be detected.

* I will make every effort to be a good ambassador for all metal detectorists so that I leave a good impression when ever I detect.

Etiquette to Other Detectorists

You will inevitably run into other detectorists. Don't be afraid to say hi and admire their equipment. You may get an offer to try it out if you want. Its a great way to sample another machine.

Its fun to compare notes and most importantly, learn from other MD hobbyists.

When you are in the same general area with another MDer, try to give each other some space. The last thing you want to avoid doing is come up behind them and start detecting where they just finished. They probably wouldn't appreciate you pulling up the find of a lifetime right in the same spot they were 3 minutes ago… There is plenty of space in this world so there is no need to be right next to them.

The exception to this is if you are out with a friend of yours. You may want to be somewhat near each other, just not following in each other's trail. Often my friends like to call me over to a signal with the offer of "see what you think about this one". Its great to compare notes on what you each think the item will be once its dug up. A little competition is good too. It can help motivate you to dig more (and find more) targets.

The bottom line is just be courteous when you are out there. Common sense should prevail and if something "seems wrong" to do, then it probably is wrong.

One example that comes up in forums now in then is whether it is legal or ethical to detect in cemeteries.

Just the fact that someone is questioning it in the first place should be a red flag to them. Legalities aside, the mere perception that you are in there digging up where deceased people are buried should be a clue to avoid doing it.

Plus many people leave mementos and coins on graves. Do you really want to be the person in there collecting coins left behind for someone's dead family member. No. I didn't think so. Again, common sense should prevail. There are too many other good places to detect in this world without leaving a bad impression of our hobby.

Etiquette to the Public

When I am out detecting I try to be as discrete and respectful as possible. A big part of that is making sure I am wearing my headphones. When people are out enjoying nature, they most likely don't want to be hearing the beep... beep... beeeeeeeeep of your detector.

Be courteous and spare them that unneeded noise.

Along the same lines as that, give people plenty of space. If you are at a large open park or beach, there is not any need to go right next to someone and start detecting. Imagine yourself at the beach, eyes closed on your blanket only to start hearing a metal detector by your head. You open your eyes and there is someone swinging their coil a few feet from your head.

Common sense, I know. Unfortunately its a scenario I see all too often.

When you are interacting with strangers, it is in all of our best interest to be friendly and help educate people. I always make it a point of showing off all of the trash I had collected so far. Most people have no idea the ground is filled with pull tabs, nails and bottle caps. Judging by how interested they are, I may give a impromptu lesson on how to use the pinpointer.

Building a good rapport with people will not only keep people's opinion about our hobby great but it can also lead to invitations to dig at new locations.

CHAPTER THREE

The Hunt is On!

Where to Detect

There is a famous quote attributed to bank robber Willie Sutton. The legend has it when asked why he robs banks, he replied "Because that's where the money is". Willie denied in his autobiography that he ever said that, but its a great quote.

For metal detecting, the question could be "Why do you detect at beaches or parks? Because that's where the money is… and rings… and valuables…".

The longer you are in this hobby, the more you detect (pun intended) good spots that are likely to return some good hidden targets.

The obvious choices of where to detect do include beaches and parks but there are many more to consider. Once you start thinking about anywhere that people gather and hang out for a bit, the more opportunities you realize there are everywhere around you.

There is a way to tell when you are really getting hooked on this hobby. As you drive or walk around, you are going to start observing all landscape. You'll start analyzing the potential for detecting there and/or guessing about what may be hidden just under the surface.

Here is a list of places to consider detecting and the most common items you are likely to find there. For some of the more common locations, I am going to elaborate on specific tactics in a moment.

Parks - Coins, Jewelry

Beaches - Coins, gold and silver jewelry, cell phones, matchbox cars... you name it.

"Tot Lots" - (Children playgrounds) - Coins, jewelry, matchbox cars.

Old Farm Houses - Old coins, relics

Ballfields - (Especially under bleachers and side lines where parents would set up chairs to watch). Plenty of coins (and bottle caps, pull tabs...).

Old Abandoned Properties or Foundations - Coins and relics.

Trails - Coins, possibly relics (depending on how old the trail is). Keep in mind that some trails these days started off as wagon trails or walking paths over 100 years ago.

Fairgrounds - Coins and occasional jewelry. Don't forget the parking lots. Lot of packing and unpacking of cars with items spilling out.

Rivers and Streams - (Swimming and fishing areas) - Coins, rings, ear rings, bracelets, fishing items like lures, hooks and weights.

Under Ski Lifts - Coins and cell phones. "Wow great view up here. Let me pull out my deeply buried cell phone while wearing these thick ski gloves that offer terrible dexterity!". By the way, many phones and cameras have memory cards. Even if the phone is junk you can sometimes pull out a 64GB memory card worth a few bucks.

Bus Stops - Coins and lots of pull tabs.

Site Seeing (scenic pull over areas, airplane runway viewing spots) - Coins, pull tabs, bottle caps, can slaw...

Old Picnic Groves - Relics, old coins.

Battle Sites (from any war or skirmish) - Relics, old coins.

Stone Wall Property Boundaries - Relics, old coins, Jimmy Hoffa.

Grass between the street and the sidewalk - Coins (including a surprising amount of older silver ones).

Bridges or Trestles - Coins, caches.

Large (old) Lone Trees or stumps - Coins, caches.

Old Camp Grounds - Coins and nearly anything else

is possible.

Snow Sledding Hills - Coins, jewelry.

Please remember to check with your local state and town ordinances to make sure there is not any prohibition on detecting in these spots. If its not public property (or prohibited) then you need to get permission to detect on private lands. I'll cover the best tactics on doing that in an upcoming chapter.

Some states actually prohibit you from detecting at the beach or at certain parks. When in doubt a phone call to the local town office or park department will clear up the issue for you.

The main reason metal detecting gets banned is due to inconsiderate MD hobbyists. People who leave unfilled holes or are loudly beeping their machines next to people trying to enjoy the area. Some courtesy and consideration goes a LONG way.

I often take out a pouch full of beer caps, pull tabs, nails, shredded aluminum cans and much more. I also make a point of showing anyone curious enough to talk to me about my hobby. That way they can appreciate that I am out there making a difference in the environment, not destroying it.

Now let's take a look at some specific tactics and considerations for the most popularly detected areas.

Getting Permission

If the idea of finding antique relics and very old coins is appealing to you, then you need to strongly consider metal detecting on private land. You will likely get the benefit of having access to virgin territory which has never been detected yet.

Some of my metal detecting friends focus almost exclusively on detecting old yards, fields and property. They rarely, if ever, venture into public parks or beaches.

Please remember you can only detect legally on land that you have permission to be on. Don't assume a place is legal to detect on, including the beach. Some states prohibit detecting even on public beaches. Thankfully those are few and far between but it is up to you to double check.

If you are unsure, Google is your friend. Simply Google in your state (or town) and terms such as metal detecting law or ordinance. Also detecting forums are a great place to search and ask if you are unsure.

Here is a rather comprehensive site which lists many laws based on location. It also tackles many MD law topics including how to get laws changed to be more favorable. I can not vouch for its accuracy and its always a good idea to double check any source. Its a good start though:

http://www.mdhtalk.org/maps/fp-map-regulations.htm

Private Property Permission

As far asking someone for permission to detect on their property, this may seem intimidating at first. It is actually surprisingly easy as long as you keep a few things in mind.

These tips below are compiled from various solid sources and also my own experience.

First of all remember this. Before you get permission, you do not have the right to be on somebody's property. So until you ask, then the answer is "No". So by asking you have nothing to lose. The only thing they can do is say no which is where you were at to begin with.

Luckily with a few of the tips below, you will get a lot more "yes" answers than "no's".

Here are some tactics that you can use to help increase the odds of property owners saying yes to you.

General Tips

Do not show up with metal detector in hand. Instead, be well dressed with no detector in sight. Otherwise you are putting them in a more awkward position. It looks you are ready to go right to work. While that may be true, it isn't a good first impression.

Don't bother approaching houses with extremely well manicured lawns. If it looks like a golf course, that homeowner is likely super sensitive about their grass and its condition. The thought of someone harming a blade of it would probably keep them up at night. Your rejection rate is typically very high at these houses.

Typically the bigger the yard the better. I like to picture big outdoor house parties from a hundred years ago with lots of old coins being dropped over the years.

Do your homework. Find out some history about the neighborhood and the age of the average house. This can give you some talking items of interest to start the conversation.

First I do some online research for a few minutes. I use sites such as www.historicmapworks.com

I find some older maps with my target area on it and print out a few copies. I like to have this in hand when I talk to the property owner. Offer them a copy while you explain why this area is interesting to you.

I have found that the weekends can be a great time to

catch people outside. They may be washing their car, working on the house etc.

My pitch is similar to the following. It is modeled after a similar approach that a very good detectorist ("CTTodd") uses. Todd has his own Youtube channel with a username of CTTodd1. He does incredibly well finding old colonial coins and pretty much sticks to private property (with permission) locations.

"Howdy! (with a big smile on my face) I am not here to sell anything, I just have a quick question.

My name is Tim, and I live right here in town off xxxx street. I am a bit of a history buff and I love older neighborhoods and property such as this. I have a hobby of metal detecting where I search for old relics in fields and old property. Anything in the ground can catch my interest. If something is interesting enough then I offer it to the local historical society" (which is true).

"I find the stuff using a modern metal detector. You've probably seen those before being used at the beach or at a park. "

You'll notice that I avoid talking about old coins or treasures. Mentioning those puts property owners in the wrong mindset. They then start thinking "what valuable thing is this stranger looking to take from my yard". Downplaying things as rusty relics helps to lower that sensitivity level.

"Do you think it would be okay if I detected a bit of your property at some point?"

A common response at this point is "Sure. Go for it".

Some may want to know more details however. I can then elaborate depending on what they asked. Some points I may mention based on what they ask include the following.

"I would use my detector to locate small lost objects. They are typically only a few inches in the ground. They are removed with great care in a way that make it nearly impossible to even know I was there. If I find anything particularly interesting, I'd be happy to show you if you want. "

Quite often I do get a yes at this point.

If so, **"Are there any days that would be best?"**.

Most people don't care. The typical answer is "whenever you want" or "anytime is fine". If they are fine with me giving it a try now then I will thank them and go back to the truck to get started. Its polite to ask if its okay to be parked where you are in case they have a preference.

Tip: When getting started, consider beginning away

from their house initially. Slowly proceed closer and make sure you are taking extra care with the holes and plugs. They will likely periodically take a peak out to see how you are doing. Once they realize that nothing exciting is happening and that you are conscientious about your digging, they are likely to not even bother watching much anymore.

If they turn me down, I thank them anyways. I respect their right to say no. Usually I reply "Okay, no problem. It never hurts to ask and I sincerely appreciate your time".

Tip: I have found that having my 9 year old son with me, increases the odds quite a bit in my favor. Instead of 7 out of 10 yeses, it is more like 9 out of 10. I explain this is a hobby that the two of us enjoy doing together. It definitely helps break the ice even faster.

Sometimes you will get property owners who are legitimately interested or fascinated in the process. I take the time to explain things and let them try if they want. You are now doing them the favor by catering to their interest.

Tip: If they are really receptive, it never hurts to ask if they know of any other properties around here that may be worth trying to detect. If they are older, feel free to have them reminisce a bit about places that they used to like to hang out as a kid. Favorite fishing holes, picnic spots or perhaps parks that are now abandoned. All of these are solid leads worth following up on.

Done correctly you will often not only get permission but invitations to come back anytime.

Detecting Tips for the Park

This is probably the number one place most detectorists start off at. There is a good reason. It is public, detecting is usually not prohibited and there is a fresh supply of new lost items pretty regularly.

By the way, the term tot lot most often refers playground areas for very small kids. Usually if there is bark mulch or shredded rubber underneath playground equipment, it is probably a tot lot.

Between tot lots and parks, they are a great way to get a lot of experience. They are also a good choice to start off with when you want to introduce kids to metal detecting. There is usually some change to be had to keep their interest.

When looking at a park, the obvious places to hit include:

* The parking area and grass leading to/from the park

* Under and around benches, picnic tables and bleachers

* Shady trees

* Underneath low hanging branches (where upside down pockets lead to spills)

* Stumps or ground impressions where shady trees

may have once stood

* Under and around the swings / hanging tires / jungle gyms

If the park is still in use, my advice is leave your shovel in your vehicle. Instead a hand trowel like a Lesche tool is a lot less intimidating to people walking around in a well manicured park. It's extremely important that you learn the proper way to dig plugs especially the park. Last thing you want this to be drawing attention to the fact that you have left all the holes all over the place.

There is also the technique called coin popping which can greatly hide the fact that you were ever there in the first place. I cover the proper way to dig plugs shortly.

Remember to take any trash that you uncover. It is the polite thing to do. Believe me, people are watching you whether you realize it or not.

You don't have to worry about minding your own business. There are plenty of people doing it for you!

Another etiquette consideration is to make sure you are using headphones. People trying to enjoy the park really don't want to be hearing "beep… beep… beeeeeeeeeeep" the whole time they are there. Help preserve our great hobby by leaving a good impression.

Be Prepared: Pull Tabs

Remember those old style pull tabs that were meant to come off a can when opened? If you don't remember them, you will soon enough! Those old style tabs are EVERYWHERE.

The newer style tabs aren't meant to come off too easily but you will stand find plenty of them too.

You can set many detectors to discriminate (not alert) to pull tabs, but you do it at a big risk. You will also not be alerted to many types of gold jewelry. Unfortunately they can register about in the same range.

Quite often if a signal is alerting in the pull tab range, it will alternate between a pull tab and one notch above or below it. As I repeatedly swing it back and forth it keeps hopping between two notches on my detector. More often than not that is a sign of a pull tab or trash. If I am being picky, then a solid repeatable signal is a good sign for me to definitely dig. Keep in mind different model machines may react differently. This is one of the important reasons to really get to know your machine by putting in the hours with it.

Pro Tip: A site which is mostly older style beer can

pull tabs may hint at the age of things there. The old types which was meant to be pulled off went the way of the dodo bird in the late 1970's and early 1980's.

When you are detecting you want to be paying attention to such things. If you are into finding older coins, this is a hint that you are in an area that was popular at least that long ago.

By the way, don't let the pull tabs get you down. You are helping to clean up a bit. Besides its my personal philosophy that each pull tab recovered gives me one more karma point towards finding the big mother lode cache someday.

Whenever we dig another pull tab, my son likes to say "Oh no! Our nemesis. The pull tab!". My reply is "Yes! Another pull tab. We are one dig closer to a gold ring or coin."

Pro Tips:

#1) When looking at the variety of parks to choose from, I like to do just a few moments of research first. In particular I like to look back in time.

I do this by taking a look at the park "then and now" by using Google Earth.

Google Earth is so useful to me that I have a separate chapter in this book covering just that topic. It is a great way to view what the park look like years or even decades ago. By using it to "go back in time" you can see what changes may have happened at the park. Including what wooded parts (now) may have not been wooded decades ago.

#2) When you have decided that metal detecting is for you and not a passing fad, then you may want to consider investing in a smaller coil. These are great for trashy areas such as many parks. By trashy, I mean there is a lot of beer tabs and caps just under the surface. This can make it a bit frustrating after you have dug up your 12th pull tab in a row. A smaller "sniper" coil or a 5"x8" coil can help you pinpoint valid targets that may be very near to trash items.

I use my sniper coil very successfully in one of my favorite hunting parks. The park is out of the way but was very popular 100 years ago. While it is immaculate to the naked eye, just under the surface is a LOT of aluminum, trashy objects. Many a beer can's content have met their demise here over the last hundred and fifty years or so. While I don't find many cans, I do find many of the pull tabs that used to be on beer cans. A smaller coil lets me hear the silver barber dimes that are lying near a pull tab.

The sniper coils are also fantastic for getting into hard

to reach places. They can go much closer to metal structures before sounding off. Their beams are more focused so you can get right next to park bench legs, swing set poles etc.

Most parks are hit fairly often but only a small percentage get into the hard to reach places. I am often pleasantly rewarded when I bring my sniper coil to poke around.

For me personally, I like to hit parks at off peak times.

#3) I have a tactic for larger parks as well. If I find that the common areas are already well hunted out, then out go to the outskirts of the park. If other people zig, then I zag. Hit those areas that most detectorists never get around to. They either are so fixated on the common areas or they give up when they believe the park is hunted out.

I have found many great finds "off the beaten" path a bit. Usually in an area on the opposite side of the popular places to detect. Many great finds have been found doing this by looking in places others never got around to checking.

Don't be afraid to venture off into the woods or bushes. The less convenient it is to get to, the less likely it is that a casual metal detectorist before you has gone there. Keep in mind that just because there may be obstacles there now, it doesn't mean that was the case 100 years ago.

I have hit some great finds underneath a dense bush or pricker brush plant. Again, that plant hasn't always been there. It is doing a good job now of deterring the novice metal detectorist from getting under there. You are on your way to being beyond novice however with this tip alone!

#4) If you time is limited and you won't be coming back to the park, then be sure to pay attention to the shaded areas. The shady (eastern) side of trees for example. Also the places where people would set up to eat lunch.

If there is a stage or band shell, then picture the thousands of people over the years who have spread out their blankets to watch the performances. This is a good place to find jewelry in addition to coins.

Concession stands at ball fields can yield dozens of coins after a busy weekend of ball games. Many of the coins aren't even buried so keep your eyes open.

#5) For a park that has a volleyball or basketball court, that would be my first stop. Sweaty hands making fast, jerking movements is a great recipe for losing jewelry. I know some people that focus a lot of their effort just on searching volley ball courts in their area. Judging from their reported finds there, it is a habit paying off nicely for them. With the price of gold as it is, it doesn't take too many rings to more than pay off any metal detector.

#6) Be sure to talk to people. Help educate them about the benefits of what we do (cleaning up). Show interested kids if their parents are okay with that. Once I've built a bit of interest and rapport, I like to say something like "Its a lot of fun detecting at an older property such as this. I am always on the look out for a new place to give it a try so if you know anyone with an old property that might be a good fit, I'd be really grateful to hear about it". You will be surprised what leads may turn up. It may be as simple as "well, our property is only 1/2 an acre but it does date back into the 1800's. You are welcome to stop by" or "I know someone that you should talk to…".

You never know until you ask.

The more polite and sincere you are, the more people want to help you.

#7) Under and around picnic tables is an obvious place

to want to detect. Keep in mind however that unless the table is permanently mounted, they may in fact change the positions of them from time to time. Keep an eye out for grass wear patterns. Between not getting much sun under the table and people's feet wearing out the grass, usually there are clues to where tables used to be. Be sure to hit those spots too.

Detecting Tips for the Woods

When talking about my favorite places to go detecting, I like to get off the beaten path. Actually on the beaten path as well.

I am talking about the opportunities for true treasures to be found in fields and the woods. Some places that a beginning detectorists may not initially give much thought to. After all, there are not a lot of people there all the time.

It amazes me the discoveries that can be found seemingly in the middle of no where. It is not unusual for a metal detecting club to pick a nice quiet field in a tucked away town to hold an event. Often to the land owners amazement, they uncover coins from 100, 200 and even 300+ years ago.

That is just in the U.S.

Go to Europe and the finds go back even further.

What may seemingly be a remote spot now, may have been a hub of activity hundreds of years ago.

Old walking paths, or even better, wagon paths might have been the "highways" back in the day when no other roads existed.

Just a few weeks ago a MD friend of mine invited me

to his dad's farm field to detect with him. The field had recently been plowed to make way for upcoming corn crops to grow. It was about 15 acres of gentle rolling hills with row after row of recently plowed lanes. For someone new to detecting, it would seem like the last place to try out.

It was actually pleasant searching there because there were very little junk signal hits. I did find some various tractor bolts and nuts but after about 20 minutes my friend started waving to get my attention. I walked over and he showed me the coin he just found. A 1737 copper.

He explained that he has found several other old copper and silver coins in this very field the last few times he's tried it. He then explained that the farms here were over 200 years old. In all those years, farmer after farmer had tended to the crops in this field. Along the way they have inevitably dropped some coins.

Lesson: you will start viewing old property with a much more appreciation in this hobby.

Besides fields and farm property, I like searching wooded areas as well.

Here are some of my tips when you are out scouting out the woods for good spots to detect.

This is where your detective skills start coming in.

Much like Sherlock Holmes, you are paying attention to the subtle things that no one else might give a second notice to.

Rock / stone walls - These are commonly used as boundary lines especially on older properties. If you find yourself deep in the woods and a rock wall appears out of no where, this is a good sign that there was some sort of settlement nearby.

I like to detect along rock walls, making sure to check right up to and on the wall itself. It took some hard work to get those rock walls in place. It was a good opportunity for them to drop some coins while they were working on it. It is not unheard of to find an old coin spill along a rock wall. As good as finding an old coin is, finding several in the same hole is pretty hard to beat.

Stone walls are also a great spot to look for relics. Its not unusual to find old bottles, tools, utensils and pretty much anything else that may have been discarded years ago.

Old Stone Cellars - This is a real good spot to slow down and take a look. Finding the remains of the foundation of an old house from 150 to 200 years ago can yield some very interesting finds. It may not look like much. Just a bunch of old stones outlining where a house used to be. There could be a treasure trove of old relics and hopefully coins there as well. It is not uncommon to find old buttons, utensils, bells, thimbles, locks and was as coins from the 1800's or earlier. Be sure you scan the walls of the foundation themselves. Old coins and items have been known to be tucked between the rocks in their little hiding spots.

Few things get my MD heart pumping like being able to detect on an old cellar hole that was recently discovered.

Be careful of where you are walking. Many older homes have wells for water for both the occupants and their animals. Often these have been covered up with rocks or debris. Some can be quite deep and its definitely not something you want to find by accident.

Old tree stumps - ALWAYS detect thoroughly around old (especially large) trees and tree stumps. Trees are like people magnets. We are drawn to them to sit against, swing off of, have picnics under and even stash some valuables now and then. Because they are such a good landmark, it is a natural choice for people wanting to hide something that they wish to eventually find again.

I have found plenty of coins under tree roots, under the tree itself and even in the wood of rotted out stumps. That is why its important to scan every square inch.

"Reading Trees" - If the tree is still standing take a good look at it. Not just down but up.

Is there signs of a rope having been wrapped around it at some point? That could indicate a clothes line possibly. If that is the case, follow the line of where the clothes line lead. Coins fall out of pockets when they are hung up on the clothes line. If you do find some coins, there may be quite a few in the area so it is well worth digging every promising signal there.

Finding Buried Caches - A 100+ years ago it wasn't easy or convenient for most people to keep their money in banks. Many people didn't trust banks either. For good reasons in some cases. Because of this is was not uncommon for property owners to stash away valuables in a buried caches.

Often times a property owner wanted to keep an eye on their cache, for obvious reasons. Having it buried within eye sight of their house gave them an added peace of mind.

One tactic used by farmers would be to bury the cache at the bottom of a fence post hole. Odds are the cache would not be any deeper than the farmers arm. The cache could be placed then some dirt and then the fence post. Just like the dozens of other posts fencing in their properly. Pretty good way to mark it and no one is suspicious about the digging activity needed to put it in place.

Another tactic used to mark a cache location can be seen on trees.

Do you see a nail or spike in the tree or a branch? They would tie a string with a heavy object (as a "plumb bob") around the nail. Where it hangs above is a good place to search deep to see if there are any signs of a buried cache.

Detecting at the Beach

When most people think of metal detecting, they may envision someone at the beach slowly checking the sand.

If you are lucky enough to live within driving distance to a beach, it is can be quite a pleasurable way to spend a few hours. The sights, the sounds, the feeling of sand underfoot… and of course the potential finds there!

The beach is a very attractive target to detect because it can be a never ending supply of coins and jewelry.

The beach has so many conditions which are ripe for people losing valuables. Activities such as:

* lying down on their blankets (coin spill out of pockets)

* taking off jewelry to apply sun tan lotion

* having slippery lotion on fingers, hands and arms letting jewelry slip off

* playing in the sand

* cool water shrinks the skin on fingers, loosening rings

* throwing footballs, frisbees or spiking volleyballs

can fling rings off sweaty fingers

* clearing the sand off of blankets inadvertently leads to flinging jewelry into the sand

So many opportunities for you… so little time!

The thing to keep in mind at the beach is that there IS jewelry to be found. Now is not the time to be setting your metal detector to ignore (discriminate) against certain targets. The reason is that a lot of gold rings up in the same ranges as junk like pull tabs. If you ignore pull tab signals, you are also ignoring possible gold jewelry.

Beach Searching Tips

Pay attention to where people generally lay out at a beach. Quite often there is a line of towels with in about 20 feet from the high tide mark. At our beaches I can tell the high tide mark due to a bit of seaweed that is the furthest up on the beach. Quite often people are just above that line on the dry sand.

I make it a point of searching all around abandoned sand castles or holes in the ground. Quite often parents are over helping kids do some digging and its a good spot to check.

For a digging tool, I have a sand scoop. There are a wide variety of them available from hand held to long handled scoops. I prefer a long handle scoop to save myself from bending down any more than I have to.

My scoop has a metal handle and has 1/4 inch mesh screens in the scoop portion. This allows me to shake the scoop to sift out sand but keep in the goodies. I bought my first one on eBay for under $50. I have since upgraded to a much larger "T-Rex" scoop which cost over $150. A basic scoop is fine to begin with.

When I get a signal, I pinpoint where it is and how deep it is. I like to remember the read out numbers and guess what it is that I am about to dig up. I recommend you always do this to help sharpen your skills with your machine.

Once I know that I have pinpointed exactly over the target, I press my coil down in the sand slightly just to make an impression where the target it. Think of it as a bulls eye that I can refer to if I take my eyes off of it for a moment.

If the target was reading very high up, then I will use my Pro Pointer to find out where it is. I can then use a non-metallic scoop to scoop up the target. The plastic hand held scoop is great because I can use the pro pointer or detector to scan over it without the hand tool itself being detected.

If the target is deeper than a few inches then I position the long handled scoop and push it into the sand with my foot. Once I scoop I then scan the hole to see if I picked it up or not. If so, then I dump the sand to the side and spread it out with my foot. Often I will see the item right then but if not my detector or Pro Pointer will quickly locate it.

I don't carry my long handle sand scoop. Instead I have a small bit of rope tied to it and it clips onto my finds pouch. I then let it drag behind me as I walk. This not only makes it so I don't have to carry it but more importantly, it leaves a trail behind me. That helps me see where I have been and makes it very easy for me to avoid going over the same sand twice.

If I am trying to get a feel for where most of the targets are at I will do some W shaped walking patters from the soft sand down to the water line and then back up again. I am paying attention to where I am getting hits for legitimate targets. Often these will be clustered at certain levels and it helps me to focus on detecting more along that stretch of beach.

Its a good idea to keep an eye on the tide charts for your beach. You can easily find that by googling it.

Wet Sand Tips

When you transition from the dry sand to the wet sand, be sure you ground balance your metal detector if it has that capability. This allows the detector to sense the new environment and set itself up to have as little false signal as possible while being as sensitive as practical.

If you are planning on doing some water or wet sand hunting, I recommend hitting the beach 2 hours before low tide. That gives you about 4 hours of good hunting in the wetter environment that will soon be underwater. This is the area that people will be playing in the water a few hours later. This is some prime spots to be losing rings and jewelry.

Pay attention to the sand conditions. Look for low spots in the sand where perhaps there are small puddles of water. Also the areas on some beaches where water actually forms "cuts" in the sand. Searching in those lower areas is a good tactic for potential items.

If there is a decent amount of small pebbles, pay attention to how they are bunching up at certain spots in the sand. Coins may also be getting drawn to the area or a few feet behind it. Its worth walking down that line to see what may have accumulated there.

After Storms - One tactic popular with experienced metal detectorists is to hit beaches immediately after storms. The bigger the storm the better.

The waves which get stirred up can really shift sand around. It can help uncover portions of the beach that

may have previously been under several feet of sand.
Look at the beach line or dunes for sand that drops off
like someone came by with a bull dozer. Waves and
wind can carve away tons of sand leaving some long
lost goodies waiting for you. Make sure to give those
areas a good detecting, including the sides of the
"cliffs" that have been cut away for you.

Sand Sweepers - One of the beaches I like to hit is
cleaned every night by a tractor sand sweeper. It
comes by and scrapes the top layer of sand and uses
brushes to catch the trash.

On first impression this seems like a very bad thing for
metal detectorists. After all, it is scooping up all of the
dropped items right?

Not necessarily.

The machines are designed to grab pieces of paper,
cups and larger items. It OCCASIONALLY will snag
a necklace or bracelet on one its bristles but it is not
clearing out the beach from all of its goodies. A friend
of mine worked 2 summers driving the machine and he
said it was pretty rare to actually find anything good.

The caveat to this is that there are different models of
"beach rakes" or sand sweepers. Some are more
thorough than others. The one I am used to is not very
thorough as far as small items go.

Now here's a good tip concerning these.

Go to where the machines turn around to make another pass at the beach. The curves of their paths are great places to detect. Especially the inside and outside of the curves. The reasons is due to the snow plow type effect of these sweepers. They can push sand (and items in the sand) in a slight plowing fashion. When they make the turn, the items get pushed to the sides of those curves.
That is always one of the spots I like to hit on my rounds to the beach.

This photo shows what I am talking about. This was taken this week. Since it was 80 and sunny, I figured I would hit the local beach first thing on a Monday morning. I was glad I did!

Notice the tire marks in the sand. That is the sand sweeper that came through around 9 o'clock last night. The arrows show my digging spots first thing this morning. I retrieved quite a few clad coins as well as a diamond stud earring. Well, at least I thought it was a diamond at first until I saw the backing was cheap metal so it more like a cubic zirconia.

This photo brings up another good point.

Once you have hit upon a target rich area, then really search the heck out of it. Slow and overlapping your coil swings. You will usually be rewarded for the extra effort.

As far as the sand sweepers, you should also see if you can tell where they empty out their loads. Sometimes the go around the corner (perhaps around a dune) and dump or transfer their garbage into trucks. This is a good area to detect once they have cleared out as well in case anything small fell out while they went about the transfer.

Web Cams - If I know I am heading to the beach the next day, I will keep an eye on the local beach web cam. It is a camera that shows the beach in real time.

Many beaches have web cams these days. You can find them by Googling the name of the beach and then the words web cam. So for example:
Laguna beach web cam

Don't be surprised if there are multiple cameras for popular beaches. I bookmark my favorite ones in my browser for easy future reference.

Some of the cameras switch position every 5 to 10 seconds so its worth watching to see if that happens.

I will take screen shots of any interesting areas that I may see. I pay attention to large groups of people who may be in a particular spot. I also note any locations that people are playing volleyball, football etc.
The next day I make sure to head for those spots first upon arriving.

For taking screen shots I use a program called Snagit (www.snagit.com) but there are plenty of other free screen capture programs available that can do that.
I will email myself any really good images so I can refer to the EXACT location when I am at the beach.

Several times I have been glad I had the image to refer to so this is a recommended strategy to try.

Here's an example. If I was headed out and saw this screen shot:

To the top right is one of the many entrances to the beach. I would park right there and then go straight for the spots where those groups are. The top right most group are playing volleyball while the others are groups of 10 to 20 people in each group. That would be an excellent starting path for my trek the next day. By sending this photo to my cell phone I can refer to land marks if needed.

If I hadn't looked at the web cam, it would have not had that information.

Beach Courtesy

I mention this in the etiquette section but its worth repeating. Please be courteous to other people on the beach by wearing your headphones. There are not too many people that went to the beach with the desire to listen to your machine beeping. Also give people who are laying or sitting down plenty of room. Don't infringe on their personal space by swinging your machine right up to where they are.

Beach Cautions

Keep in mind that most metal detectors are NOT waterproof. Some have coils that are water proof but their control boxes are not. You want to make sure whether yours is or not before getting it wet in the surf.

The Garrett Ace 250 is waterproof all the way up to the housing box. I don't recommend taking it out in the surf however as it is probably just a matter of time before you either drop it, get hit by a stray wave or lose your balance. The result is a wet control box and a possibly ruined machine. Digging in water can be tricky and a balancing act so don't tempt fate.

Some machines are made for all terrain, including the water. Examples of that include the Garrett AT Pro, Minelabs CTX 3030 or Excaliber II.

Even if your machine is waterproof, it can be a bit more challenging. Salt water is conductive and because of that can lead to false signals. The same goes for wet sand. It is important to ground balance your machine when ever you switch from dry sand to a wet environment.

Each machine ground balances different. As an example, the AT Pro has a button for it. You hold your coil just off the ground in a spot without any targets. Then press and hold the ground balance button. With the button held, you "pump" the coil up and down about 8 to 10 inches several times until you hear any noise die down. Make sure you are bring the coil down as close to the ground as you will be scanning the ground at.

You can then further tweak the ground balance if you want either a little more or less depending on your tastes. By doing this you will have a lot less false signals in the wet sand or water. Don't forget to ground balance it again once you transition back to dry land again.

If your machine is water proof and you want to try it out in the water, use common sense. Only do it when it is calm. It is challenging enough with wave action, trying to scoop and scan. Don't be putting yourself in any dangerous surf or rip tide conditions where it would be nearly impossible to MD successfully anyways.

I wouldn't recommend going in too deep either. I've seen some people detecting in neck deep water. That doesn't leave a lot of room for error if you lose your balance or you have some sort of issue where you need help.

Detecting Tips for Old Property

Once you get tired of parks and new coins, you will start to realize that detecting on older properties is very desirable. More old coins and excellent relics are found in private yards and fields than pretty much anywhere else. More often than not, you may be the first person to ever swing a metal detector over their soil.

When you do get permission to detect on someone's property, you likely don't want to over stay your welcome. That means that you want to detect the property intelligently. Focus on the areas most likely to produce finds quickly for you. If you do have unlimited time there, all the better but still start with areas with the most potential.

First things first is to focus on making sure you make a good impression. This can be the difference in "hey come back anytime you want" versus no invitation to return.

Make sure you have gotten good plug cutting and coin popping techniques practiced. There is a chapter in this book specifically on that. Don't make someone's private yard the place where you learn how to do it. Sharpen your skills in your own yard first.

Okay now that you are ready to get started, here are some tips to maximizing a hunt on private property.

* Front yards are generally used a lot more than back yards. Specifically the paths to and from the doors of the house. Detect there before the backyard.

* Find out where old out buildings used to be. Sheds, barns, outhouses, wells… The paths to those areas were high traffic and hold good coin potential. Look for clues about where things USED to exist. Look for old brick walkway, paths in the lawn or woods or any other signs that something used to be in that direction which may not be there anymore.

* Get under the front porch if possible. Many a coin have likely slipped through the cracks. Imagine all of the times someone has reached into their pocket to grab their keys only to have a coin bounce down there.

* If there are sidewalks, check right along the grass edge. Coins like to bounce and land next to side walks, including in the cracks.

* Look at the old trees on the property. Give them a good search. People love shady spots as well as climbing branches, and stashing goodies near roots.

* Look for signs of an old clothes line on trees. There may be a circle of bark where a rope had been embedded years ago. Check where the clothes were hanging out to dry for all of the goodies that spilled out of the pockets. Anyone with a modern washer or dryer knows how many coins turn up there. Same concept for a hundred years ago with clothes lines.

* Pay attention to clusters of trees, especially if they are in a row. These are often intentionally planted years ago to offer shade and wind protection to a building. Its a good hint to check that area.

* If the property is on a corner lot at an intersection, pay attention to where people would naturally cut across the lawn to shorten their trip. Often they won't cut across a full yard but the last 10 to 20 feet before the corner may be fair game for people looking to literally "cut corners".

When you are done with the property make sure you leave on a good note. Also ask if they have any suggestions for other old places to hunt in the area. If they can refer you to a friend or neighbor then you are almost guaranteed to get permission there as well.

If you had a particularly productive dig, consider giving the property owner a small token of your appreciation. Perhaps a silver mercury dime or something else as a thanks.

Detecting Tips for Fresh Water Hunting

I love fresh water hunting, especially in and around lakes. Compared to ocean hunting it is usually quieter with calmer and warmer water. It also does not involve the false signals that salt water hunting can introduce to many metal detectors.

While many people are land locked without an ocean within hundreds of miles, nearly every area has dozens of fresh water bodies. Most of those have some sort of impromptu beach or swimming hole.

There are many sites which map out where swimming holes are located. Here is an example of one: http://www.swimmingholes.org/

There is a map where you can click on a particular area to see more details.

First Things First

Before you dip your machine in any water, be sure to check that it is a waterproof model. Some models like the Garrett Ace 250 are only waterproof up to just before the control box. Its fine to get the coil and stem wet but you don't want the box getting wet. Some machines can't be used at all in the water, so again check first.

My Garrett AT Pro is 100% waterproof with the optional waterproof headphones. Oddly enough they don't come standard with waterproof headphones which is a bit irritating to find out if you didn't know that before hand.

I can literally swim underwater with my headphones on. Up to 10 feet down. Sounds adventurous right? The reality is I rarely stick my head underwater. It is nice that I can simply drop the machine in the water without worrying about it getting wet at all though.

Sandbars

Most locals on bigger lakes know where the social sandbars are in the area. That is where boats can anchor up and then everyone can jump out into water that isn't over their heads. On my lake the sandbar is THE hot spot on warm weekends. There are actually boats there every day but on say the 4th of July, there can be nearly 100 boats all circled around, boat bump to boat bumper with folks enjoying the water.

Here is an example of one of several in our local area. The sand bar is only knee high deep water at the shallowest part. The boats pull in as far as they can. Then the jump out to anchor.

The boaters are slicked up with slippery sun tan lotion, jumping into cool water (shrinkage!) and playing various activities. Many are drinking beer or their favorite Summertime cocktail. All of this leads to coins and jewelry coming off. Sometimes clothes too but that's a story for another day.

Since the Summers are short in New Hampshire, I take full advantage of sandbar time and try to get out there at least once a week if not more.

Its a great way to cool off on a 85 degree day. As an added benefit, the sights aren't too bad either!

The general mood at the sandbar fluctuates between

relaxed to partying. All depending on the time of day or groups present. Either way it is a bunch of friendly people which makes for an enjoyable hunt.

Ground Balance

This is important and worth mentioning again. As soon as you change any environment with your detector, you should ground balance it if has that option. So going from dry land to dry sand to wet sand to water and back again… all of those are times to ground balance. This helps make sure the machine is not returning false signals and is getting the maximum depth possible for the condition you are detecting in.

For machines which have the feature, you should refer to your owner's manual or youtube on how to properly ground balance it.

See More Clearly

It can be a bit challenging at times to see either your coil and your sand scoop when it is underwater. Even in the clear waters where I detect, the sand gets kicked up and can cloud things for a few moments.

To help with visibility, I bought some yellow duct tape. I put a bit of tape on the front edge of my coil. I also put some on the top, front portion of my T-Rex 8" sand scoop. This helps me to quickly orient the scoop in the right direction when the water is a bit cloudy. Before doing this, sometimes I would find myself bringing the scoop in backwards for a moment before realizing it was spun around. The tape pretty much makes it obvious if I am doing that.

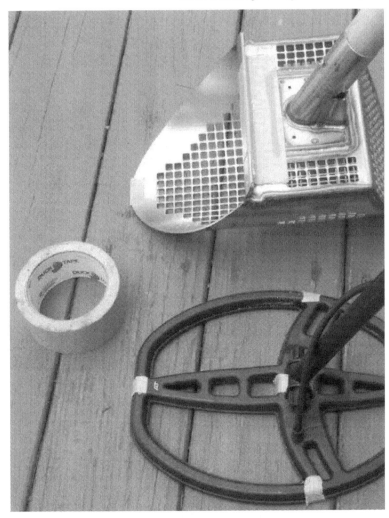

Here is the tape that I use. It is right around $4 for yellow. They have it in a rainbow of colors but I figured yellow is probably about the most visible for underwater:

http://amzn.to/1ta3IEC

Underwater Recoveries and Pinpointing

This can be a challenge until you get some good practice in. Even in clear water it can be a bit tricky initially getting a feel of where to dig.

My technique is to use the pinpoint mode on my Garrett AT Pro. I hold the button and find the strongest signal. I then slowly pull the coil towards me until the signal drops off. That tells me the target is just off the front edge of the coil.

I make sure that I note how deep the machine is indicating. If its only 2 inches then I know I can simply skim the top of the sand to collect what ever is there. If its deep however then I have to point the tip of my scoop at a steep angle. For deeper targets, I visually note where the signal dropped off. I then move the coil back another 6 inches or so and hold it there. Then I line up the tip of the scoop off the front edge of the coil and dig deep.

I slowly push down on the scoop handle so it is prying the sand up. I make sure not to have the scoop's contents coming flying up (and out) of the scoop. For deeper water I will use my right foot to put it under the scoop handle, near the bucket head. My leg will then slowly help move it over a couple feet to my left of where I just dug. It has to be far enough away that the detector doesn't give false signals from the scoop's metal.

Scan the hole and if it is still in the hole, dump the scoop underwater and go for another scoop full.

Rescan the pile that you had dug up once you have located one target. Coin spills are very common in the water. I often find other coins in the scoops of sand that I had just dug out a moment ago.

When I am done, I give a bunch of the sand a push back into the hole.

I strongly prefer to wear sandals while water detecting. Between pushing the scoop with my feet and walking on rocks, I like having the protection. The sandals I have are waterproof and appear to be made from old recycled tires.

Focusing on Jewelry

When I am water hunting at local beaches or sandbars, I am typically not going after relics.

I don't go after any iron signals at all. Any relics or bottle caps are getting ignored as much as possible.

My focus is not on recovering clad coins and pennies.

Instead, I usually am zeroed in on jewelry as much as possible. Digging up some coins will be inevitable and happens a lot. Its just I am more focused on gold and silver range tones.

On my AT Pro, gold comes in at a range that foil and pull tabs also comes in at. I dig those signals especially if it is a solid signal that doesn't vary too much on my detector's read out. If it is jumping all over the place, it is very likely to be junk. If it is in the same range within a number or two repeatedly, then it is definitely more promising.

This picture below are just some of my finds from the last couple of weeks of water hunting. Rings, bracelets, pendants, charms and earrings are common items to find. There were PLENTY of coins as well as pull tabs etc. The picture gives you some idea of what is definitely possible in a pretty short amount of time. That is assuming you are focusing on jewelry and also have a spot where people do (or did) frequent at some point in time.

"Ring in the scoop!" is a great feeling each time it happens.

Scoops

Once you know for sure you are hooked on water detecting, you should strongly consider getting a good water scoop. I originally started with a long handled sand scoop and it was adequate but just barely. It was taking me several attempts to scoop up targets once I pinpointed them. I was also at risk of breaking it constantly.

Finally, I invested in a T-Rex 8" water scoop. It is built like a tank. I could literally drive over it and doubt it would so much as flinch.

The T-Rex scoops up about 3x as much content as my old scoop. I keep track of all of my hunts and have confirmed that I am digging up a bit more than 3x's as many targets due to the speed of it. I quickly increased the rate at which I was finding good items like rings. While not cheap (over $150) it was a great investment.

The competitors to the T-Rex include the Stavr (made in the Ukraine) and the Stealth scoop among others. Here is a link to a page which has various scoop manufacturers and where to buy them: http://metaldetectingforum.com/showthread.php?t=14 2698

I like the T-Rex because it has a wider top "lip". That is the portion of the scoop where I have a strip of yellow duct tape. I often see items that I am lifting up go fluttering about in the scoop, only to be caught by the width of that top lip. If it wasn't there, I have no doubts I would be chasing more targets now and then that made their way out of the scoop. Its not essential to have but I am glad my scoop does have it.

Prime Digging Spots

When at any body of water, pay attention to what the water is doing to the elements around it. In particular, is sand or small pebbles being built up in a certain area? The same forces which are accumulating those small pebbles also can affect coins and jewelry.

In fresh water I look for ripple lines in the water. Take a look at this picture. Notice the distinct line of pebbles along the short line. This is where they settle in from being pushed by the incoming waves. Its not just rocks you will find there.

Here is another shot along that same beach with wavy ripples. Besides checking that whole area over, be sure to detect over incoming streams. That is the top arrow in the next picture.

If anything had been washed down stream at all, it
may end up getting pooled where other debris is also

building up. Mother nature doesn't know a rock from a ring so the same effects of physics can apply to both.

Some heavier jewelry may be a bit more difficult to move. That includes heavy gold rings but they can often be found in or approaching those areas. They may have sunk in to the sand before making it all the way so its worth giving those surrounding areas a good working over with your detector.

Planning Your MD Day

My apologies ahead of time.

A lot of this may seem like common sense but I wanted to share with you my thought process prior to heading out on a MD trip. It may give you a few things to think about as well.

First off, I have a duffel bag in the back of my truck. Here are some of the supplies I keep in there:

* Bug spray

* Knee pads

* Hat

* Baby wipes

* Sunscreen

* Duct tape

* Root saw

* Magnify glass and Jewelers loupe

* First aid kit with band-aids and basics including benedryl and caladryl for bites and stings

* Tecnu poison ivy soap (clean hands and equipment

of oil immediately upon exposure)

* Snacks (granola bars and a bag of resealable almonds)

* Bottles of water

* Shop rags (for clean up and also for putting dirt on when digging plugs)

* Rain coat

* Finds pouch (utility belt I purchased from Home Depot)

* Digging tools

* Digging gloves

A note about my digging gloves.

I prefer to use a digging glove on my non-detector hand only. I hold my detector on my right side without a glove. When I do use a glove on both hands then my detector hand obviously gets all dirty. The face of the detector can get scratched if I am using a glove caked with dirt. It also gets the handle and machine dirty in general. For that reason I prefer to keep any hole digging to my left hand.

Since I only use my left hand glove, I have a stock pile of right hand gloves. If you are in need of large right hand only gloves, let me know. Just kidding. Sort of. Maybe there is a market for that somewhere!

I prefer to use some nitrile gloves that I bought at WallyWorld (Walmart). There was a 3 pack for about $2.97 I believe. I know other detectorists who spend $10, $20 or more for one pair of gloves. I don't even like those better than my nearly $1 a pair Walmart specials!

The business side of the glove and fingers has a rubber coating. The back side is a cottony type fabric to let my hands breath a bit. I do not get the glove which is ALL rubber coating. Otherwise my hands would be more sweaty than a seal in a wet suit!

Here is a picture of one of my well used left handed nitrile gloves. It is hard to beat that price so I have extras available at all time.

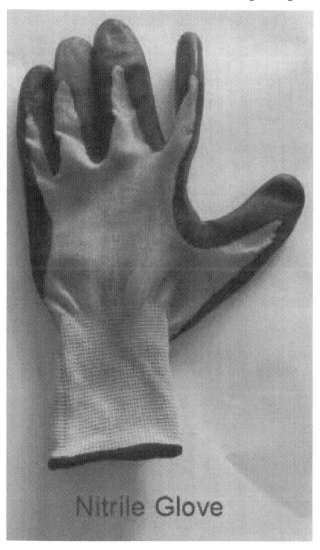

Nitrile Glove

* Extra AA and 9V batteries (for my detector and Pro pointer)

I keep several sets of replacement batteries in my

truck. I also keep one "pack" of them with me while detecting. You need to protect the batteries from shorting out. Particularly the 9 volt battery. If any metal touches both connectors at the top it will start shorting and causing a hazard.

Here is how I protect my batteries once they are out of their packaging.

First I lay out a strip of duct tape to place the batteries on. The duct tape is handy to have out with you in case it is ever needed. There isn't much duct tape can't do for temporary fixes. Not only am I protecting the batteries as seen here but I can use that duct tape in an emergency.

Note that I covered the 9 volt battery with a bit of additional duct tape as well.
Once it is wrapped in one direction, do the same thing with another piece of duct tape in the other direction like this:

Here is the finished package. They are then put inside a sandwich sized ziplock bag to protect them from moisture. I consider this my "emergency" bundle of batteries. Normally I will refill from the extra set in my truck. If I need to away from my vehicle I have these. The reality though is it is usually my friends borrowing my batteries because they forgot theirs!

Here is a look at my typical yard / wood digging set up:

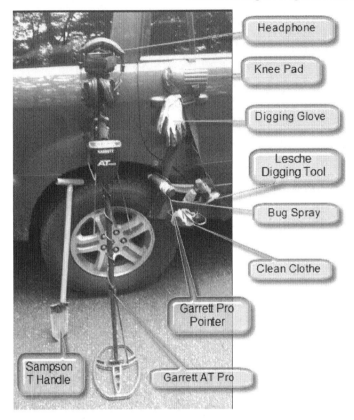

Strategies

The night before I go out detecting, I review the weather. In particular the temperature and chance of rain.

If its going to be a hot day, then I try to avoid the main hours of the sun. I will also plan my detecting route accordingly.

As an example, this morning I had picked out a small pond near me. My research had uncovered that this pond was created by the town about 150 years ago as a water source. It is a fairly large pond and I wanted to focus on the areas that were likely in use back then.

In looking at the weather, it was going to be sunny and in the mid 80's

That meant an early start for me. I wanted to avoid the hottest part of the day if possible.

I jumped on google Maps to zoom in with the satellite view (http://maps.google.com). I like to do this prior to every new hunt location so I can familiarize myself with the location before I get there. It is not uncommon for me to spot some interesting looking areas or structures that I want to make a point of checking.

Zooming in I could see that the area was partly wooded and then was more open along the water's edge.

Upon arriving I made sure I started doing my initial detecting in the unshaded area first, while it was still cool. That way as the morning heated up, I could escape into the shade of the woods.

I also brought along my ever present can of bug spray. I keep it in one of my utility pound pockets for a quick spritz when ever the mosquitoes start to make their appearance.

Permission

If I am detecting in a public area of a new town, I will research to make sure I have the proper permission. Often googling the town name and these words will uncover if there is any particular town ordinance concerning metal detecting. So if it was "Anytown, CA" I would google:

Anytown ca metal detecting ordinance
Anytown ca metal detecting law
Anytown ca metal detecting permit

Besides actual related ordinances, quite often it will turn up any recent town meeting references concerning metal detecting. When in doubt, call the town offices. Don't be surprised if it takes a few transfers of calls before you get anyone who knows what the real story is!

Be sure you note who you talked to and their phone number in case you need to refer back. If they sound suspiciously like they don't know what they are talking about and then tell you it is not allowed, politely ask how you can see the applicable rule online. You may be dealing with someone who doesn't really know and doesn't want to bother finding the truth. No matter what, always keep it courteous though.

If I do find a related town ordinance, I make a copy of the website URL as well as the text of the ordinance. I use a free app called Evernote (www.evernote.com) which I then paste it into. That app shares its information with my computers, ipad and cell phone.

So paste it in one device and they all have a copy of it. Its handy to be able to pull up that information on demand if the need ever arrives.

TIP: One thing I've learned from experience is that if I have a particular spot in mind that I want to hit, I make sure I hit that area first.

In the past I have started detecting before I walked to the area of interest only to be distracted and run out of time. By at least hitting the region that got my sixth sense tingling first, I can make sure that part gets covered before I have to leave. This is also true of spots where you know people will start to arrive later that day. For example I sometimes detect near sandbars where boats congregate. If I want to detect along the anchor line (where they line up) then I will make sure I hit the most popular spots there first. Later in the day they will be occupied by "new depositors". That is the boats will start showing up and blocking access from those spots.

CHAPTER FOUR

Taking Your Detecting to the Next Level

A Collection of Real World Tips

As you get some detecting time under your belt, you are (hopefully) starting to concentrate on getting even better at it.

There are some people who are very, very good at metal detecting. You may attribute that to their high end fancy machine but you would be surprised. They can do quite well for themselves with an introductory level machine like a Fisher F2 or Garrett Ace 250.

An expert with a beginner machine will out perform a rookie with a high end machine just about any day.

Here are some of the traits that separate the rookies from the pros. You've already taken a big step by reading through this book but there's more to do.

Experience. Okay this is an obvious one but it can't be over stated. You WILL get better over time, so it is important to put that time investment into it. Time with your machine will reward you with learning its personality, its quirks, strengths and weaknesses.

The best way to get some good detecting time in is to hit some local ball fields or parks. You will mostly be hitting clad (modern) coins but it will be excellent experience for you to get the hang of how your machine is reacting.

Dig Everything. Until you get many hours of experience I recommend you dig everything but before you do... make a mental note of how it is registering on your machine. Is it a steady indication or is it jumping all over the place? Was it as deep down as the detector indicated? You should be guessing BEFORE you dig what you think the item is. You will start having a better and better success rate identifying things before you dig them up.

Dig everything you hear for at least the first 20 hours or so. One VERY big "secret" of extremely successful detectorists is that they dig nearly everything all the time. The exception is those targets which are obviously too big to be coins (like a can or large chunk of metal). That can be determined with pinpointer practice.

Do you want to find valuable gold jewelry? Then its absolutely essential you dig even those signals that you think are pull tabs.

One way to know you are on the right track to finding gold jewelry is by digging up nickels and pull tabs. If you aren't digging those up over time then you are being too picky with your signals and you are missing out on chances for some valuable gold rings.

Here is a very good Youtube video which specifically

Metal Detecting for Beginners and Beyond

demonstrates this. He compares several different types of gold rings along with various junk like foil, pull tabs, bottle caps.

https://www.youtube.com/watch?v=6P-AtJJYdOw

Watching that will really drive home the fact that you need to dig everything if you want gold.

Over time you can decide that you may want a day where you ONLY coin shoot. That is you are not focusing on relics and perhaps not too concerned about finding gold either. In that case you can be pickier as to what items you want to dig up. On my machine I can set it to ignore (discriminate) on everything except dime, quarters and silver. In a really trashy area this will help to only alert me to those coins. Will I be missing other items? Yes absolutely but it may save my sanity if I just want to go out and try to find some old silver or even regular clad coins.

Discrimination can be bad - Most detectors allow you to discriminate certain signals from sounding. For example if you don't want to hear iron targets, you can "discriminate out" the iron. When you detector senses that, it won't alert you with a tone. It is important to note that discriminating out ANYTHING can affect good targets as well at times. When you tell your machine to ignore certain targets, it will do so but if there is a valid target right near it, the machines processor may not recover in enough time to report the good item. The result is simply a block of both good and bad items.

So the rule is, use the discrimination feature cautiously and realize it can negatively affect picking up some legitimate targets as well at times.

Most of the time, I prefer to detect with zero discrimination. After a while I mentally tune out the low iron tones and am only listening for mid or higher tones.

RTFM (Read the friendly manual) - Be sure you've read the owner's manual. No, no. I saw you skim through it. I mean READ it (please!). Multiple times if necessary. It can contain little nuggets of important information.

I recommend rereading it after you have a dozen or two hours under your belt as well. It may take on a whole new meaning now that you have had it live out in the field.

Also jump onto youtube and search for your model detector. Pay attention to some of the tips and tactics shared specifically for your machine.

If you are itchy to metal detect but the weather is not cooperating, then use some time to get on Youtube.

Watch the successful hunters who are using your machine. Some are very good about sharing tips about their specific machines in a variety of conditions. This is a great way to get to know your machine's subtle personality better.

Experience will teach you how to use the pinpoint feature on your detector more precisely. This is really imperative to make your digs more accurate. This translates to more objects dug up as well as smaller plugs or holes that you have to dig.

As you are learning, pay attention to how accurate your predictions are. Once you dig up the target, make a mental note if it was directly underneath the middle of the plug or you were off to one side. Also note how deep your machine said the target was versus how deep you actually found it. Repetitive practice will really help sharpen your skills. If you aren't paying attention to these factors then you are not gaining nearly as much from this practice as you could be.

Swing Slowly - One thing that helped me considerably was to really, really slow down my swing speed with my AT Pro. If I can see it moving, its going too fast. Well, kidding but close. Once I started slowing down I started realizing I was missing a lot of signals, especially deeper ones.

A fast swing will typically have no problem detecting coins near the top of the surface. Deeper down or smaller targets are another story. Slowing down also lets you sense one target then let your machine have a split second to recover. It can then report the next target which may be lying right next to it.

The day I finally got this through my thick skull was a record setting day for sheer number of coins recovered. I realized after that the VERY quick, faint high tones I was hearing were actually often legitimate targets. Slowing way down let those targets become much more obvious to me.

Important point: Most detectorists seem eager to cover as much ground as possible. Change your mindset. Make it your goal to cover as much ground as THOROUGHLY as possible. This is partially accomplished by using a slow swing speed.

Join a Club - Flatten your learning curve. Just as you are learning tips in this book that will help you, getting with experienced detectorists will also help you out considerably. Use google to find metal detector clubs in your area. Typically they meet every month or two. They often organize hunts together on property where they have been granted permission. These events are a great way to learn from some dedicated people. You can also check out different machines, tools and first hand tactics. Don't be afraid to ask for help. That is what it is all about.

Here is a link to many clubs in the U.S., the U.K. and Canada: http://www.metaldetectingintheusa.com/metal-detecting-clubs.html

General Tips and Observations

Here is a look at some things that can separate a novice detectorist from a very proficient one. The are kind of wide ranging but useful to get you beyond the pure beginner stage.

REALLY Covering An Area

If you find a particularly good search area, then it makes sense to thoroughly search it for other targets.

To do this as completely as possible, create a small are of say 10 feet x 10 feet and SLOWLY work over it. Make sure you are overlapping your coil swings by about a 1/3 each time. It is important to know that the signal going down into the ground is shaped like an ice cream cone. The deeper it goes down, the less of an area is is picking up. By overlapping your coil swings, you are maximizing your potential to find as much there as possible.

One you have covered that whole area going say east/west and back, then do it from north/south and back.

You will often find signals going in one direction that you didn't hit on going the other way. If a coin is laying vertically in the ground for example it can be nearly invisible in one direction versus the other.

Also if there is junk iron near a target and you are discriminating out iron, then it can mask (hide) the presence of the good target. Hitting an area from a different direction can often reveal the good targets that you had missed coming from another direction.

It is practically impossible for an area to **truly** be hunted out completely. Someone with more finesse and/or a more advanced machine may be able to find targets that others have passed by.

Take Advantage of Change Events

Every so often there are events that literally change the landscape. They can be man made (construction, excavation) or created by Mother Nature (floods, hurricanes).

If you see a paving crew tearing up a road or sidewalk, it may be the first time in 70 years that the dirt underneath has seen the light of day. If you are going

to act, you need to do it quickly. Typically they will
tear it up one day and then come back the next to pave
over it again. If you miss that window of opportunity,
it will likely never open up again in your lifetime.
Talk to the work crew there about the schedule. If they
tearing it up on a Friday, they likely won't be back at it
until Monday. Quite often that section may be closed
off to traffic in the meantime...

Another example of man made events is clearing an
old lot for the first time to prepare for construction. I
found an interesting area near me that had old mills
from 150 years ago. I went to check out this town
property only to discover that they very recently had
removed the top soil. I was very disappointed as it
seemed to hold some real promise. This is what I saw:

On a whim, I started detecting the mound...

Sure enough I recovered some old coins in the dirt
pile. I started talking with one of the construction

foremen about it and he found it interesting. He offered to knock down the pile a bit with his backhoe and spread it out for me a bit. Offer accepted!

Be Prepared - One piece that may eventually fail on your machine is the bolt which holds your coil to the shaft of your detector. That pretty much puts an end to that day's activities. Unless you are prepared for that of course!

I ordered a back up bolt for my machine. It is duct taped underneath the cuff of my detector as shown here:

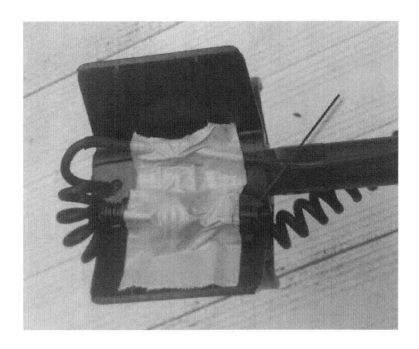

I can also use that duct tape for an impromptu repair of something else as needed.

For a few bucks it is worth the peace of mind to have this part on hand. Just in case.

It is invisible to me normally as it is underneath my elbow on the under side of my arm cuff.

Storms

Seasoned metal detectorists often perk up when they know a big storm is headed to a beach near them. A big storm means big waves and winds. They often literally change the landscape. What used to be covered by 6 feet of sand now has mere inches of sand. Dunes which have been there for years are suddenly carved open for exploration.

Some of the most frequent Spanish coin finds on Florida's "Treasure Coast" happen with days of a large hurricane blowing through the area.

Learn to stay tuned to such happenings. They will take on a whole new meaning now that you are metal detecting.

One really good spot to check on the beach only presents itself occasionally. It is a good one to know about.

Look in the shallow parts of the beach. Pay attention if you see something that almost looks like a sandbar in the very shallow surf. In particular if the water pulling back to the ocean is rippling on the land side of that shallow sandbar. If you look closely you would likely see small rocks and debris being pulled back to the ocean but hitting the land side edge of that ledge. The water ripples and flows over the edge towards the ocean but heavier items get trapped on the land side and sink. This is a great place to detect for trapped coins, rings and jewelry that is also getting trapped there.

You won't see that all the time but when you do… score!

Good People to Know

I just mentioned a construction foreman I befriended. Construction workers in generally are usually pretty personable, hard working guys and gals. I have found a lot of them love the outdoors which is why they are doing what they do. A high percentage of them are hunters and fishermen.

They often love swapping stories when the action is a bit slow. It helps pass the time a bit.

After explaining my hobby, I usually hear "I always wanted to try that". I then explain the desire to find old property such as farms, fields, stone walls and cellar holes.

They have provided some great tips on cellar holes that they remember from hunting. They've also let me know about upcoming construction projects that I could get a day's worth of access to.

I was talking with one about how much history must be at a very old, large private school in town. The school dates to the late 1700's. I said it was a shame all that history is being scraped off their grounds every time they put up a new building. He then said, you should go detect where they dump all of their top soil. He then went on to describe (in detail) exactly where in town that was. He then offered up the name of the person who I could get permission from to do it.

Sweet!

It was (and still is) a productive site.

Snow Bound Tip

I live in New Hampshire. Lots of snow and a few months without good detecting weather. It is a sad story so I won't dwell on it.

Here is a tip for you if you are in a similar climate.

Pay attention to where they pile the snow mounds in

the winter time. You guessed it. Those spots make GREAT places to detect once the snow melts. Those plows have been scooping stuff all over town and have conveniently deposited some of them right there for you. Give it a scan. You may be pleasantly surprised.

"Looking for Gold? Look for Old"

One of the blogs I follow is from someone who gets a LOT of silver coins. By a lot, I mean several hundred a year. A few years back, he found over 1,100 silver coins in one year.

He explained that one of his success tactics is to take as many different routes as he can when he is driving somewhere. He intentionally takes side roads and indirect routes to check out various properties. He is specifically look for "signs of old". Old grass in particular. Grass that hasn't been grated over or filled in. After awhile you will start being able to recognize old versus new grass.

Old grass: uneven, bare or brown in spots with clumps of weeds or wild bushes here and there.

New grass: built up, fluffy. Ball field looking.

He logs all of his "old grass" observations then goes door knocking for permission to detect there. This one tip alone could propel you into metal detecting greatness if you really focus on it.

A Picture is Worth a Thousand Words

When at the local library, ask if they have copies of old yearbooks. Many of them do.

Flip through and look at the pictures in the year books. In particular you want the outdoor shots. Schools used to take class shots outside by tree lines, walls etc. Imagine all of these fidgety kids waiting to have their pictures taken. Hands in pockets, then out of pockets bringing some coins with them.

Look for playground photos as well. Pay attention where they are located as they often change over the years. This can help you zero in on a playground area from 70 years ago that is no longer in that spot. This can lead to some nice silver coin discoveries.

Any locations then, which are different now, can be good hints for you.

Protecting Your Detector

It is not a good idea to leave your metal detector in extreme temperatures. It is an electronic device and can be affected by it. This is especially true in heat of summer. Having it stored in a trunk or direct sunlight is not a good idea. A variety of bad things could happen including the screen "rainbowing", components and/or batteries melting as well as the possibility of theft from the vehicle. Generally if you would not be comfortable in the environment then do your detector a favor and don't leave it there either.

Its also a good idea to periodically wipe down your detector with a slightly damp cloth. Sand will get in around joints and screws. If your machine is water proof then give it a good rinse, particularly after visiting salt water. Its important that the connector ports are free of dirt and sand. On a water proof machine, having sand in those spots can break the seal and let water leak into the control box.

Easy on the Eyes

To make it easier on my eyes, I carry both a magnifying glass as well as a jewelers loupe. That is the small magnifier that you would see a jeweler inspecting a diamond with.

I bought this 3 pack of jewelers loupes for under $8.

http://amzn.to/1mhpaSs

They are probably not "jeweler approved" but they work great for me. Because they give three, my son gets to keep one in his pouch while I have one with me as well. I keep the other at my house for looking at items after the hunt.

A BIG tip for looking at teeny tiny dates is to use natural sunlight. Even simply tilting the coin towards a lit window can make a big difference in making things more readable. Sounds simple because it is. It is also not always immediately obvious if you aren't used to doing it.

I also have a secret weapon. My 9 year old son has eagle eyes. He can see dates with his bare eyes which I have a hard time seeing sometimes even with the loupe! He has been right every time so now I just trust him on it.

What's in a Name?

Start paying attention to street names.

"Back in the day" they were descriptive. Maps were rare so Mill Street obviously ran by the mill.

Other examples include variations of these:

Church street
Railroad Ave
Grove road (picnic grove or tree grove area)
Falls road (former mill location? Swimming hole?)
Bay road (swimming hole, beach)
Park street
School street

They all were usually indicative of what was there. If that type of structure isn't there now, even better. You have a lead on finding out what was there and more importantly where it used to be. That is a great lead for detecting in a potentially lucrative area.

Street names will take on a whole new meaning now that you are metal detecting.

Cornerstones

If it is an old public building that you are detecting (like a school or a church) look for cornerstone blocks with a date on them. It will give you indication of when it was built. Also turn to google to research the properties history as much as you can. I found mid 1800's school which I did some research on. The building was still there along with a cornerstone from 1861.

In researching it, one article mentioned in passing that some dirt from the school was moved a few hundred feet away to help prepare for new baseball fields that were built about 20 years ago. Turns out old coins were transferred during that move as well. The outskirts of the ball fields suddenly became a lot more interesting place to hunt.

Botany

You may end up learning many new things with your metal detecting hobby. One of them should be a bit of botany, or the study of plants.

In particular, poison plants.

Poison ivy, sumac and poison oak.

Do yourself a favor and learn to recognize the leaves of each. You are bound to run into it while detecting and you want to stay clear. If you are not sure what they look like, head to Google Images: http://images.google.com

Search for each and you will see many example photos.

I always thought I was immune to poison ivy. I actually tried getting it at 12 years old on a bet. I was fine but my best friend wished he didn't try it as well. This year my luck changed. I got it for the first time in my life. I spent a few miserable, itchy nights with it. It took about 2 weeks to go away. I bought a few lotions at the pharmacy which did help but I am not looking forward to repeating the experience.

I ended up cleaning all of my equipment and clothing as I wasn't sure what day I had come in contact with it. To be safe, I cleaned it all.

I used Technu for getting the oil off of myself and my equipment. Then I used IvaRest to stop the itching.

Both of those were in my local grocery store pharmacy sections.

Keep Your Secrets

If people see you keep detecting one spot too many times, it may likely be sending the wrong signals. They will know you probably found a "honey hole". Learn to keep a low profile. If you do feel the need to keep hitting the same place repeatedly, consider varying your times or day of the week.

If they ask, you can tell them you are looking for lead sinkers and old shell casings to recycle. That is probably one of the most boring answers a detectorists could get and is not likely to motivate them into competing.

The last thing you want to be doing is posting online any hints at particular good spots. I GUARANTEE that it is just a matter of time before you motivate multiple other detectorists to show up and help clear out that location.

Along the same lines… I never brag about what I found that day if a passerby asks. Usually "lots of pull tabs and bottle caps" is a typical response. You don't know who you are talking to. Bragging about the 3 silver coins you found in the last hour could lead to a lot more people hitting that spot. I also like to say with a kidding smile "I can't tell you that! Its bad luck!".

Sometimes at the beach people will half joke along the lines of "if you find a gold ring, I lost one". I will reply with "what does it looks like and what inscription is on it? I will keep an eye out for it". That usually gets them laughing or admitting they are only kidding. The last thing I would want to do is pull out a few rings from my pocket only to have them suddenly "realize" that they had lost one of those.

False Signals

This is the "what the heck is wrong with this thing?!?" chapter.

One thing that can lead to some frustration is too many false signals. That is your machine is beeping for no reason at all. It can be happening when you are standing still or swinging the coil. With experience you will learn how to minimize them.

This chapter is designed to help shorten that learning curve. These are from my own personal experiences of how to troubleshoot if your detector seems to be acting up.

You Are the Cause

When you are out detecting, its a good idea to not have steel toed boots. Even the metal eyelets for shoelaces can make your detector go off. So pay attention if you happen to keep getting beeps if the coil swings a bit close to your footwear.

Remember to keep other metal objects well enough away as well. That includes your digging tool and any rings/watches/bracelets that you may wear. I don't wear any when I am out detecting. I've had false signals that were driving me a bit nuts until I've sheepishly realized that I was setting it off by something I had with me.

Improper Swinging

You want to keep your coil as close to the ground as possible without touching. An inch or under is ideal. It is inevitable that you are going to bump the ground from time to time. This can cause your detector to sound off a false reading.

Another aspect of swinging that can cause false signaling is a swinging motion that is not flat to the ground during the whole swing. A common beginner mistake is to swing the coil back and forth like a pendulum. While most of the side to side is level with the ground, on either end of the swing, there is a tendency to swing it up off the ground. You want to avoid doing that. Your coil should be the same distance above the ground through out the whole swing.

Moisture

If your machine is not completely waterproof then

some moisture in the control box of your detector can make it act up. Mine was going crazy one day. Even simply holding the coil off the ground still had the read out registering ghost signals all of the place. It sounded like I won the jackpot on a slot machine.

It turned out that some moisture from a VERY light rain must have made its way into the housing of a non-water proof machine I had. I shut down the machine and let it dry. It was good as new.

This brings up a few good points worth repeating.

Some detectors are fine getting their coils wet. The Garrett Ace 250 is one of those. It is NOT rated water proof for the control box however. Usually higher end machines can offer that as option. In the Garrett family, the AT Pro model is waterproof. There are other benefits as well but generally the intro level detectors are not waterproof.

Here are some water resistant improving tips if your machine is not water proof:

*Apply water proof tape to the seams where the the cover of the control box is.This will help minor water from sneaking in there.

* Inside the control box you can put one of those small silica anti-moisture packets so if it does get damp at all it will help absorb the moisture.

* A control head cover is a good investment. I bought one for about $12 and put it on if its starts to drizzle out.

Another erratic signal cause is a loose connection. Make sure your cable is securely screwed in to the control box housing.

Dying batteries can also make things act up sometimes. I like to have at least 2 extra packs in my detector duffel bag at all times. 2 packs of AA's for my detector and 2 9v backups for my Garrett Pro Pointer.

Speaking of batteries, if you change yours and it starts acting up, make sure they are properly oriented. My friend had that happen just a couple of days ago as one of his was pointed the wrong way.

Electro Magnetic Interference

Sources of power or electronics that transmit can disturb your metal detector. It can interfere with its ability to accurately tell when there is an object to detect or not.

You will experience this for example if you are close to power lines. The power line doesn't need to be the ones you can see either. If there are buried power lines nearby, your machine can start getting really erratic.

Larger coils may be more affected by this. Also lowering your machine's sensitivity may help you reduce the false signals a bit. On the plus side if you are in a promising spot and can get your machine to cooperate, you may be hitting an area that has barely been detected. Most MDers likely just chalk up that area as not detectable. DO NOT dig in areas where you have any reason to believe there are power lines. That should probably go with out saying but I did anyways. Common sense should always prevail.

Another source of false or erratic signals can be your cell phone. Don't keep it in your front pockets. When the controls of the detector swing close enough to your pocket, it can cause some machines to act up. This is particularly true if the cell phone is actively looking for a cell tower signal or perhaps receiving a text message.

Other Machines

If you are hunting with a buddy and they are close by, your machines may be picking up each others signals. This is particularly true if they are using the same

Metal Detecting for Beginners and Beyond

model as you. Many machines let you change frequencies to select a quieter frequency to detect on which instantly solves this problem. You should check your detectors owner's manual to see if that is possible and how to do it.

As an example, on my AT Pro I hold down the pinpoint button. Then with it held down, I press the sensitivity buttons to cycle through frequencies until I find a quiet one. I had to do that this weekend when hunting with another AT Pro friend of mine.

Don't Be Overly Sensitive

Finally, if the machine seems to be a bit too erratic, make sure your sensitivity on it is not too high. Some machines are almost overly sensitive unless they are turned down a bit. My Ace 250 is one that I keep at 2 notches down from full sensitivity most of the time. I can have down even 4 notches or more and still not seem to suffer too much while eliminating false signals. You will have to experiment a bit as you learn to get used to your own machine's personality.

Raise the sensitivity until you start running into false signals. Then back it down one notch.

When you are detecting in any water (even a shallow puddle) you may want to lower the sensitivity. Water can have an amplifying affect on things.

By the way, this water influence works in your favor at times. If the ground is damp your machine is likely to be able to detect deeper than normal. This is best if you don't have a lot of iron targets (nails etc) in the area as those will be showing up more as well. Its a good tip to keep in mind after a good rain storm though. Hit some of those places you thought were hunted out and you just may get some deeper coins.

All Wrapped Up

Another good tip concerns your coil wire. That is the connecting wire that goes from your coil at the bottom of the detector, up the shaft and into the detector's control box.

Instead of starting to wrap the coil round and round immediately above the coil, try running it for about a foot straight up the shaft. THEN start coiling up the rest of the way up to the control box.

I secure the coil to the shaft using velcro bands but electrical tape can work as well. Here is a screen shot of my machine:

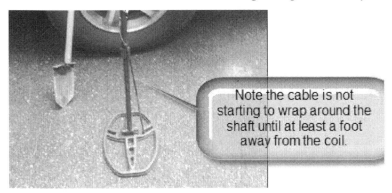

Be sure the cable is not loose or else it can jiggle and cause false signals.

These tips should help address 95% of the false signals you encounter.

If you are still running into weird issues, contact support for the machine. They can walk you through some troubleshooting to see if the coil or control box needs to be replaced.

Pinpointing Tips

One of the nice features most detectors is a built in "pinpoint" function. When you get a hit on a target in the ground, use the pinpoint feature to really narrow down where the object is.

I use the feature by first visually noting about where the detector is picking up a target. I then move the coil away from that area. I then press and hold the pinpoint button and go back to that area.

I am watching the screen as it has a strength meter on it. I move it around the area and determine where the signal is the strongest. This will generally mean the target is directly under the part of the coil where the shaft connects to it.

TIP: To further pinpoint it even more accurately, slow pull the coils toward you. When the signal JUST starts to fade even slightly, stop. Now look at your coil the target will be directly in front of your coil.

Notice the yellow tape in the picture. I keep that on
my detector for a visual cue of where the pinpointer is
finding my target when I use that trick that I just
mentioned.

This yellow tape also helps me when I detect in the
water. It can be challenging to see the coil sometimes
between dark water, sand and the sun.

It also helps my digger (aka my son :). I tell him that
the object will be buried directly below the yellow
tape.

Getting Precise with Your Pinpointing Skills

It really pays off to practice your pinpointing skills. It can help you avoid digging up some undesirable targets.

For example, cans often hit in the quarter range on a detector. However cans and quarters "look" much differently when you are using the pinpoint on your detector. A coin typically will be a very small while a can or similar object will appear be much longer (or wider) than a coin.

Watch for the maximum signal from your pinpointer when over the target then slowly move it in various directions. Get a feel for how quickly the signal drops off. If you are moving your coil several inches and are still getting a maximum, solid signal it is not likely to be a coin.

As you get experienced you will start learning how to judge this without even putting it in pinpoint mode. By VERY slowly moving your coil in different directions over the target and paying attention to the sign strength, you learn to read the situation very quickly. This only comes with a lot of practice but it is an incredibly useful skill to develop. It will set you apart from pure rookie detectorists.

Having said that, I have dug up some "can" signals only to discover a quarter spill. The quarters were spread out over a few inches which made them seem like a can. A golden rule in detecting is "you never know until you dig it".

Using a Handheld pinpointer

Besides the detector itself and a good digging tool, I consider a handheld pinpointer the next nearly essential item to have. I wouldn't bother spending the money on it the very first day but once you are sure that you are going to stick with this hobby for a while, then it is a very good purchase.

Okay, I can already hear someone asking: "But Tim, you just talked about the pinpointing feature on your detector, why do you need another separate pinpointer tool?".

Good question.

A handheld pinpointer tool like this is made to go in the hole that you are digging. It is made to poke around and... well... pinpoint exactly where the metal is.

An an example. I have a Garrett Pro Pointer.

The Pro Pointer is shaped like a thin flashlight and can be used with one hand. With a push of a button it turns on and is ready to help you find your treasure.

The closer the wand gets to the metal, the faster it beeps. When it is a solid tone, that means it is pretty much touching the metal. This all becomes incredible useful when you are digging in a hole and everything is covered in dirt, sand or mud.

It is not designed to find things more than a few inches away. Instead its a good way to find out if you are close to the target and then helps you find it exactly.

As you dig up items, you will find many of them are very hard to spot due to them blending in so well with the dirt. The exception to this is gold which seems to jump right out at you. Silver often does as well.

I use my pinpointer almost every time before I even dig. If the detector is saying definitively that the target is deep then I won't bother. Otherwise, I will run the wand across the location horizontally first. Almost like combing the ground. Just to see if the pinpointer picks up on anything. If it does, I then use the point of the pinpointer to see if I can located exactly where it is.

As mentioned, a pinpointer that I use and recommend is the Garrett Pro Pointer. It costs about $129. This is the one used by a majority of dedicated dectectorists. There are other models out there but you would not regret getting this particular model.

Here is the cheapest price on them that I know of: http://amzn.to/1nSe9xk

I already mentioned that I like to scan a spot before I dig. If it is hitting on a target, the target is just under the surface. Instead of digging up a plug of soil, you can often pop it using a probe similar to a screw driver or the tip of your digging tool. This is particularly important if you have permission to dig at a well manicured location. You don't have to bother the grass any more than necessary.

When you have sensed a signal in your hole but are having a hard time locating it, use just the tip of the Pro Pointer. Search the walls of the hole and more often than not the object is embedded there.

Making Your Pointer LESS Sensitive

Sometimes it is handy to make your Pro Pointer less sensitive. That is it would need to be closer to the source of metal before it start beeping. You will find this useful when it is going off in a hole you dug and you are having a hard time pinning down exactly where the metal is.

This tip shows how to "retune" your Pro Pointer to desensitize it a bit.

While your Pro Pointer is in the hole and beeping a bit, hold it where it is. Then turn it off then on. It is basically ground balancing itself to the environment. Since it is near a bit of metal, it uses that as the zeroed out level. Now as you move it around the hole, it will need to be closer to the actual source of metal before it starts beeping.

This trick comes in handy more often than you might think!

Making Your Pointer MORE Sensitive

This is the opposite of what you just did. This is a way of effectively adding an inch or more depth for your Pro Pointer.

This can come in handy when you have dug a hole but you are not picking up any signal yet with your Pro Pointer.

With it still on, take any piece of metal. A coin works fine. From the handle end slowly slide it up towards the tip until the Pro Pointer starts to chirp. It will likely be near the on/off button. Then VERY slightly back it off until just to the point it stops chirping.

Now while holding the coin in place, use the Pro Pointer like normal. This has the effect of making it super sensitive now.

If that explanation was confusing, here is link for youtube on how to do it:

https://www.youtube.com/watch?v=FUlewb1xGN8

If you take a look at my Pro Pointer here, you can see I have duck taped a metal ring to the bottom of it. That serves two purposes. First I can clip something on to that and attach it to myself so I don't lose it. Second I can take that metal ring and slide it up towards my on/button to super sensitize my Pro Pointer. It makes it convenient to be able to quickly do this since the ring is right there on it.

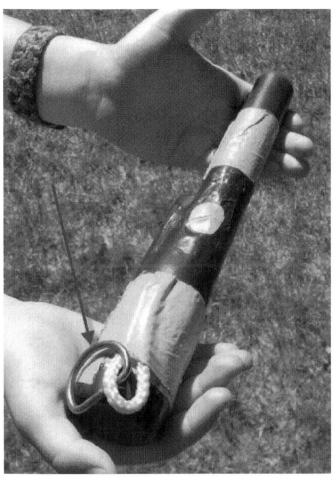

Water Proofing Your Pro Pointer

Keep in mind that most pinpointers are not waterproof.
Mine is water resistant to the point I can put most of it
under running water to rinse it off. I put my finger
over the speaker hole and haven't had any issues. I've
read from some people that they did get theirs wet but

were able to dry it out successfully. Your mileage may vary so its best to avoid testing that out!

I decided I wanted to make my Pro Pointer totally waterproof. This is how I did it but first a word of warning. I am NOT guaranteeing it will work for you and it could void your warranty if something goes wrong. Having given that caveat this is what I did:

I bought a can of "Plasti-dip" at a local hardware store. It cost me about $8 (US).

First I dipped the bottom half. That is the end that you are not holding when using it. I followed the directions by SLOWLY dipping it in and SLOWLY pulling it out of the Plasti-dip. I then waited about 1/2 an hour and I did the same end again. Finally I did that a third time after another 1/2 an hour.

The effect is that it created a durable rubber coating that does not affect the performance of the Pro Pointer. The nice thing is that I can peel off this Plasti-dip if I decide I need or want to.

Now for the waterproofing part.

I waited until the next day to make sure everything

was fully dry on the one end I did.

Then I put some electrical tape over the speaker hole.

Since you will be changing your battery every 8 hours or so of use, you will be needing to access the battery cover when that time comes. I did that by taking about 6 inches of dental floss. I wrapped the floss around the battery end and left an inch or so sticking out. This will all get plasti-dipped in a moment. The idea is that when the time comes to change the battery, you can grab this little bit of floss and unwind it off the battery cap portion. After replacing the battery, you can put more floss back in and then re-dip it. That is actually optional to do because I believe the battery cover portion is water proof. I do it just in case.

The handle end was dipped following the directions on the can. I dipped it all the way up to where the other dipping had stopped. That way the whole Pro Pointer was now fully dipped. I did that handle end 3 times just like before.

My Pro Pointer was now not only water proof but also has protective covering to protect against rock scrapes etc. The only slight down sides is that the otherwise loud speaker is now muted a bit but it still can be heard. I honestly prefer this because out in public it attracts less attention. Also the led light is covered which to me is not a big deal. I never actually used it for lighting. It was helpful to see if it was on or not but a quick wave of the Pro pointer near a piece of metal will confirm that or not as well.

Its nice having it fully water proof now. I can totally submerge it in a stream, lake or ocean without any problem. Besides regular metal detecting, it has come in handy finding items I have dropped off the end of my dock. I jump in there with my goggles on and use the Pro Pointer.

I can easily peel off the Plasti-dip from the entire Pro Pointer. It looks brand spanking new underneath.

Make It Stand Out

As you can see in the previous picture, I have put yellow duct tape on my Pro Pointer to make it easier to find. Between dropping it in fields, in the water or the mud… it helps to make it stand out.

It is ready for anything I throw at it now!

Shhh… Not So Loud

The Pro Pointer is loud. Before I water proofed mine, I put electrical tape over the speaker hole to quiet it down a bit. You don't realize how loud it can be until you are in a quiet little park and it starts chirping away. Its like the pied piper. Once kids start hearing it they start walking over like zombies to see what all the fuss is about.

I like to be a bit more discreet so even if you don't water proof it, you may want to try putting tape over that hole. You may be happy with the level of noise reduction on it.

Reward If Found

Even if you do manage to lose your Pro Pointer, be sure you have your information in it. I have a piece of paper in my battery compartment with my name and phone number. I also offer a reward for its return.

Pro Pointer Acting Up

I've read on some forums where someone's Pro Pointer can act up a bit and start giving false signals. The first thing to do is restart it and also make sure the battery is fresh. If it is still acting up take a folded up piece of paper or a small bit of foam. Open up the battery compartment and put that paper or foam between the battery and the battery compartment. This will make the battery sit a bit tighter against the connections and has resolved the issue for people.

Tip: If you are being accompanied by a child or a friend new to MDing, give them a quick lesson on using the pinpointer device. Then let them wield it as the might tool that it is. It comes with a belt holster so I strap it right onto my son Travis' pouch. He does most of the digging and between using a good digging tool and working the pro pointer, he has gotten quite effective with it.

Tip: We have a nice park near us that lines a downtown river. There are quite a few benches there. Over 30 of them.

Sometimes when we are enjoying the park, I will slip the Pro Pointer into my pocket. Then my son will give it a try around some of the benches.Simply brushing the grass will instantly turn up coins that are on or just under the surface. A small pop with short screwdriver will pop the coin right to the surface without any sign we were there.

This turns up a LOT of coins and is fun to do when you aren't in the mood for dragging out your full machine.

I credit my Pro Pointer with helping me to locate targets 3x or 4x faster.

Less digging equals less frustration. That equals more

targets you can discover.

Just recently I drove 15 minutes to a spot to detect. I realized when I got there that I left my Pro Pointer at home by accident. I drove back to get it.

That is how much it means to me.

When the time is right for you, you can get one here. It is the lowest price I've found for them: http://amzn.to/1nSe9xk

Research Tips and Techniques

Letting Your Inner Historian Come Out

Living in a very historic town in New England, I thought I knew a lot about my town's history. I now realize it was a mere fraction of what I have learned since taking up this hobby.

I have since studied many old maps, researched the local gathering spots and educated myself. I know which families were predominant in town, where the local farmers market was held in the 1800's and so much more.

All in my quest for "buried treasure" which is literally buried all around me. Don't worry if you think you live in an area with little or no history. i guarantee there is plenty of interesting and valuable things buried not too far from you either.

In this chapter I wanted to share some research tips for you to consider. These can come in handy once you decided you needed a break from swinging your detector around playgrounds!

Snapshots in Time

The art of finding old coins and interesting relics is a matter of determining where people used to congregate in your area.

One great source to try is eBay of all places.

Go to ebay.com and search for the town you are interested. In particular, search for old postcards of that town. So if you lived near Concord, N.H., search for:

Old postcard concord NH

You are likely to turn up dozens of results.

I pay particular attention to the ones showing parks, band stands and meeting areas. Remember you can click on the photos to enlarge them. I have gotten some great leads on areas by analyzing 100+ year old photos by this method. You may learn about certain parks that either don't exist anymore or were changed dramatically since the photo was taken.

I save the more interesting images for future follow up by doing the following:

* Click on the image to enlarge it.

* Use your mouse's right button to right click on the image.

* Choose "Save Image As" to save it to your computer. (The wording may be different depending on what browser you are using at the time).

I have a folder just for Metal Detecting related items. Inside that folder are other folders for towns to help keep it organized.

This is a great free resource to use to your advantage.

The Gold Mine of Your Library

If you are under 30, a library is a public building where you can go to borrow real books…

Sorry, just kidding.

Despite the power of the internet, libraries are still a wealth of information. Especially when it comes to local history.

At mine, I can access an archive of every edition of our town's paper. It goes back to 1834! Unfortunately it is still on microfiche but they are slowly working on fully digitizing it..

I like to focus on key dates. In particular editions just before and after the 4th of July. Its not uncommon to find mentions of the celebration plans and where the gatherings are happening.

Look for the names of fields, picnic groves, cross streets or landmarks. I like to target papers from the late 1800's until about 1920 or so.

While you are in there, look for newspaper editions which talk about your town centennial celebrations. So if your town was founded in 1740, look for celebrations of the event in 1840. They likely had large gatherings in different areas of town. Perhaps in a now deserted field...

Sanborn Insurance Maps

While you are at the library, ask if they have historic Sanborn Insurance Maps. These are maps outlining every piece of property in many towns dating from the late 1800's to the mid 1900's. They can be quite descriptive about the buildings and are a good resource to track down who lived where.

They plot out residential, commercial and institutional buildings as well as their outbuildings (sheds etc). Its great for locating areas where things used to exist that may not anymore.

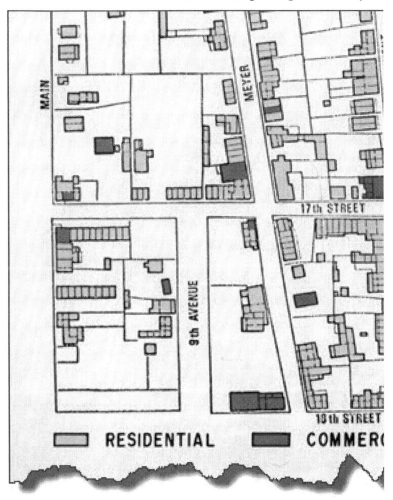

If your library doesn't carry them, its worth asking if a neighboring library does.

You can also find some Sanborn Maps online at the Library of Congress here:
http://www.loc.gov/rr/geogmap/sanborn/

They may only have references to existing maps in some cases. Often those maps are kept locally which is why its worth asking your library or even historic society about them.

Your Local Historic Society

Nearly every city and town has their own historical society. Google your town and I can pretty much guarantee one comes up. Some of the biggest history enthusiasts in an area start them up to not only track past history but to also make sure current events are properly documented for the future.

In my town the historic society resides (of course) in an old historic building. It is open a few days a week for only a few hours at a time.

They can be a wealth of information, including maps and documents that have been donated by residents. You are likely to find some information there that isn't found anywhere else. Some older residents leave some of their historical belongs to the societies. They are definitely worth stopping in for a visit.

One word of "caution". Some history buffs may view your hobby differently than you. Sometimes the mind set is that we are digging up history that should stay in the ground. You may want to hold off on elaborating on the reason for your interest in old maps until you get a sense of how they may feel about it. I know some detectorists who have gone from welcomed to outcast very quickly once it was learned they wanted to dig in the town. Your mileage may vary!

One thing to strongly consider is donating some of your more interesting relics that you may uncover in the town. If it is historically interesting somehow, consider donating it. Even something fairly mundane may be appreciated if it sheds some light on what life was like in the town hundreds of years ago.

Old Maps Online

There are several great source online to find old maps for your area. I frequently use HistoricMapWorks.com and look for maps in the late 1800's

I will slowly go over the maps and compare it to a modern map from Google maps (maps.google.com). I am looking for what properties still exist and particularly if the property is no longer there. Securing permission to metal detect on those spots is an excellent way to turn up old coins and relics.

Ghost Towns

How would you like to detect in an abandoned town where everyone fled from 100 or more years ago?

Sounds pretty cool right? Maybe a little eerie so bring a friend…

Believe it or not there are ghosts towns all over the place. Most of these abandoned towns moved due to being built in a flood zone or simply died out because the main income of the town died out.

There is a cool online site to help you find the ghost towns nearest to you. You can reach it at www.ghosttowns.com

I need your help!

I was torn between adding a lot more tips on researching location spots to detect in. My focus of this book however was for beginners / intermediate detectorist. There is more advanced information to share but I don't want to overload someone who may just be starting out.

I have been compiling more advanced tips which I can share with you, if you want.

The only catch is not monetary.

I am just looking for feedback on that project. If you are interested in getting more of my compiled tips and wouldn't mind giving some feedback once you looked through them, then let me know. I can be reached at tim@metaldetectortips.com

Proper Digging

It's extremely important that you learn how to dig up a target properly.

Rule #1 in metal detecting is always have permission to dig where you want to dig.

Rule #2 is is always fill in your holes. That includes not just in a yard but in a field, at the beach.... Etc

Many states have been outlawing metal detecting in previously legal places. It is usually based on the impression that a lot of people have of our hobby. Someone leaving holes as he goes along is giving us all a bad name.

When you dig in a grassy or a more manicured location, you want to do it in a way that respects the grass. Your goal should be to put things back so anyone would have a hard time even seeing where you had just dug up.

The key to proper grass digging is making a plug. This is like a movable cap of grass that you flip open, find your target and then flip shut when you are done.

Before you even start digging, check your target

location with your handheld pinpointer if you have
one. If it is alerting then the object is within an inch or
two of the top and a plug may not even be necessary.
If it is necessary, you should be able to make a VERY
small plug directly around the area that your
pinpointer is indicating on.

Some people dig a complete circle around the target
and remove that plug. I prefer not to do that as I think
it gives the grass a better chance of survival if you
leave some intact.

Instead I use my hand tool (Lesche digger) to cut
straight down into the dirt. Then I make a U shape
where the target is in the center of the U. After cutting
the initial shape I then work the blade around the
shape again and pry up the soil a bit at a time. Then
this piece can be flipped open with the top part of the
U being grass that is still attached to the ground.

For parks or neat lawns, I have a small shop towel I keep in my utility pouch. Basically it is about 18 inches square. Once the plug is open, I put my Pro Pointer into the hole to see if the target it right there. I check the plug as well. If it is deeper in the hole then more digging may be required. In that case I scoop out any of that dirt and put in on the shop towel that I have next to the hole.

Once I retrieve my target I recheck the hole to make sure there is nothing else. I then pour the dirt from the shop towel back into the hole. The plug is then flipped closed and I give it a few pats with my hand or shoe to seat it in place. If its grass then I will also very softly brush it back and forth to help the grass stand back up. Done properly your hole should be pretty much invisible.

A nice benefit of using the towel to shovel dirt is that it leaves a very good impression on anyone watching you. You are the likely the most neat, professional hole digger they have ever seen. Believe it or not, observations like that can help win someone over to invite you back or connect you with other dig spots.

I recently saw a Youtube video of someone digging in a park. He was finding some great old silver.

Unfortunately he was also digging holes the size of large pizzas. Not only that, he was using a large shovel to do this. He complained because the police came and told him to leave.

Between using a huge shovel and the size of his holes, it was pretty disheartening to watch it. I wasn't alone. He had posted the video in a popular MD forum. Nearly all the comments were about his poor choice of digging tools and the size of the crater he was creating. No wonder people passing by were alarmed enough to call the police. He was digging holes big enough to plant trees into. Because of that he (and other detectorists) are likely to be banned from that park in the future. Don't be "that" guy or gal.

A Less Intrusive Way to Dig

When neatness really counts (like on a manicured lawn or spotless park) there is a less intrusive way to retrieve coins.

It is called coin popping.

It works for shallow targets (4 inches or less).

Using a brass probe or screw driver, you gentle poke down into the dirt until you are actually tapping on the coin. Once you feel it, hold the probe in place then come in from the side with a long flat head screw driver. Work the tip of the screw driver under the coin and then start giving it some pops up by flicking your wrist down. Your goal is to work it to the top of the soil. The soil will bulge and then the coin will pop out. Simply pat the grass back into place and its like you were never there.

Well… at least after you get the hang of this technique.

I mentioned a brass probe. That is so that you don't scratch the target (brass is softer than most coins). Alternately you can do what I do. Use Plasti-Dip (from a hardware store) and dip just the VERY end of a flat head screw driver. Let it dry and you now have a soft tipped probe you can use.

For variations of coin popping techniques, search

Youtube for:
Coin popping

Try them out and see which one you like (if any!).

It does take some practice. Speaking of which….

Practicing

Before you go start digging up the world, pick a spot
in your own yard or an out of the way corner of a quiet
park. Do some practicing with these techniques until
you are happy with the results.

You don't want to blow your first big opportunity to
detect in a friends yard by getting it wrong. "Ahhh!
What are you doing to my lawn?!?" is not a good way
to make a first impression!

As you get used to your machine you will become
more accurate on your digging as well. That is going
to help you keep your hole sizes down to a minimum.

Nail Board Test

When you first get your machine, my recommendation is to not set it to discriminate against any metal. Even if you are primarily coin shooting, initially choose an all metal mode and dig everything.

To save your sanity, you will want to pick a non-trashy location like a field. Otherwise it will be beeping like crazy.

As you learn your machine, you are going to be very tempted to have your machine ignore iron or nail targets. In particular if you are mostly focused on coin shooting and don't care much about old relics.

There is a concern with this however that you need to know about.

Setting your machine to discriminate against nails may also hide the fact that there are coins nearby.

Metal detectors work by creating an electromagnet field. It sends it out and then reads it as it comes back from objects in the ground. Based on how the field is reacting, the machine makes a determination of what it things is causing that reaction.

A ferrous (or iron) target produces a larger change to the field. If you are discriminating out those ferrous signals, it can often hide the fact that there are some more valuable items right next to them.

Here is a way to experience this first hand.

Head over and print out this page:

http://ahrps.org/_tipsAndTechniques/Nail_Board_Test
_Scaled_to_Paper.pdf

It has an image that will fit on a normal sized piece of
paper, similar to this partial screen shot. You need to
go to that site though to get the full image.

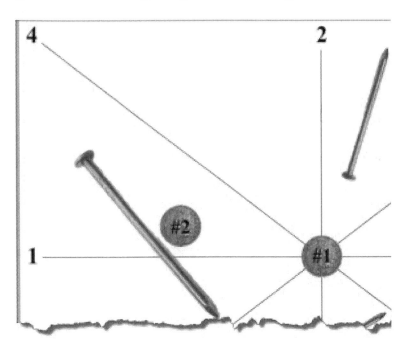

Once you print out the page, place some nails and
coins in the locations they indicated. Then test your
machine with various settings. You are likely to find

that if you are discriminating out ferrous metals, they are also not picking up the coins very clearly.

The site suggests that you apply just enough discrimination to BARELY mask out the trash. It is a good example of why you should be careful in eliminating certain metals from being detected. It can have a direct influence on something else very close by.

Having said all that... higher end machines are likely to do better with this test. That is as long as it is being operated by someone who is familiar with the nuances of their machine. Some machines are VERY good about being able to pick out targets right next to each other but this isn't something you typically find as much in a lower end machine.

My personal preference is to not discriminate out anything. I do that about 90% of the time that I detect. I am now so used to just ignoring the real low (iron) tones that it doesn't bother me. My success rate is definitely higher when I am not running discrimination.

There's an App For That

There was a time not long ago where you would want to have a handful of different tools to help you metal detect.

Perhaps you wanted access to a GPS device, flashlight, magnify glass, maps, and notebook to help. Now they all come bundled conveniently together. Even better it is in a device that nearly everyone has these days.

Do you have a smart phone? Great you are in luck! There are some very handy free or nearly free apps you can download for your iPhone or Android phone.

Here are some apps that I use pretty regularly. If you have any suggestions for other useful apps, please let me know! My email is tim@metaldetectortips.com

Your Magnifier - This is a handy app to use when you don't have a magnify glass or jewelers loupe to look at a coin more closely. It uses your phone's camera to zoom in. It can be a bit tricky on occasion to focus but

once you get the hang of it, it is useful. There is an option to take a picture of the find itself.

Price: Free
Both iPhone and Android

Flashlight - Any guesses of what this one does? Use it as a flashlight when you need it. It uses the flash on your smart phone to light up. it is very bright and I use this quite often at night.

Price: Free
Both iPhone and Android

GPS Essentials - (Android) - This is a very handy app which gives you a lot of map related tools. You can basically display a Google Map of where you are and specify different items you do (or don't) want to appear on the map.

It allows you to quickly set a way point of where you are. This is very handy if you want to mark "hot spots" to go back to later on that day or even at a later day. If you are headed out in the woods, mark your vehicles location with a way point. You can then use the app to direct you straight back to it at the end of the day.

You are also able to enter exact GPS Longitudinal and Latitude coordinates. You can use those to go exactly to spot that someone shares with you. If you get lost, you can provide that to rescuers to pinpoint you. Then again, it would be pretty hard to have this tool and still get lost... !

The main screen of this is a configurable "dashboard" where you can add or remove about 50 different items. You can put sunrise/sunset times, altitude, moon phase, bearing and plenty others.

There is also a built in compass.

If you take a picture of a particularly interesting find location, it allows you to save the GPS coordinates with the photo for future reference.

One of the features I like to use is Track. You start it at the beginning of the day and it will track a trail on the map of where you were until you stop it. Its a great way to see exactly where you were and what you may have overlooked.

Price: free
Android

Maprika - This is a very cool mapping app that takes a little bit of playing around with to fully appreciate.

It let you take any map offline and use it without an internet connection. You can also take any map and figure out its coordinates in relation to a Google Map. By any map, I mean ANY map.

So for example, if you find a great old map of your town. It likely mentions roads that have changed, have been renamed or my not even be there any more. You can specify known locations on the map as they relate to a google map. So by anchoring spots that existed then and now, as you move around in real time you can see where you are on the old map as well as on Google maps. Its very handy if you see a spot on the old map and are trying to figure out where that is now.

Believe it or not, you can actually hand draw a map and similarly coordinate it with Google Maps. They have some video examples and tutorials on their site which can help you fully appreciate this powerful tool.

Minelab's Epic - Metal Detecting Simulator for the iPhone

Weather got you stuck inside? Machine off to get repaired? Don't worry you can satisfy your need to detect if you have an iPhone. Search the app store for epic by Minelab. It simulates searching for items. Then you try and identify the item you are about to "dig up".

Supposedly they occasionally send discount coupons off equipment through the app as well. It is worth checking out if you are in the market for a Minelab machine.

http://www.minelab.com/usa/apps#epic-find

Metal Detector Organizer - I have NOT used this one as I no longer have an iPhone. It looks interesting however and it has decent reviews. The drawback is the price ($9.99) so check it out thoroughly before you decide.

It lets you track your finds via GPS. You can log them including photos. Additionally it has a built in magnifier and more.

It looks interesting and if I still had my iPhone I would probably give it a test run.

Evernote - I use this all aspects of my life. Metal Detecting included. It is a fantastic note taking, snippet collecting tool.

The beauty of it is (1) that it runs on everything. PC, Mac, iPhone, iPad, Android... and (2) what ever you enter in one device gets synced up with all of your other devices. Ironically enough I am typing this part of this book in Evernote while on the road. Once I get home, this is available to me on my home computer and other apps.

Evernote allows you to sort, archive, attach photos, audio notes and so much more. It is n incredible app and is truly my most used one.

Price: Free with affordable premium account options as well.
Available on all platforms.

A reminder. If you know of a good app to share with others, can you let me know? I am all ears! Please shoot me an email: tim@metaldetectortips.com

Power User Tip; Word of Mouth

Wouldn't it be nice to have a seemingly endless supply of new and exciting metal detecting locations lined up ahead of time?

You are in luck, because that can happen.

It simply involves getting the word out about your hobby. You need to start getting in the habit of mentioning it to people.

People are interested in hearing about metal detecting. When I mention my hobby, by far the most common reply I hear is "I always wanted to try that".

I always extend an invite but it is rarely ever taken up on. People seem to appreciate the offer though and it gives you a bit of a psychological advantage. You just offered your time to help someone try something that they always wanted to try. They are now often in a position where they want to reciprocate your kindness.

The easiest route to spread the word is to make sure your friends and family know about your hobby. Not only that but what type of property it is that you are looking for permission to search on.

When you are actually out detecting is a great time to

help spread the word. People are naturally curious and if you appear approachable, many times people will.

Kids in particular seem fascinated with what you are doing. Many are trying to figure out what is going on. Once you let them know you are looking for buried treasure… well their parents may have a hard time peeling them away from watching you.

I have 2 of my own kids under ten years old so I am sensitive to parent's protectiveness towards their kids. That is completely understandable. Usually they come wandering up and will stand 10 feet away and watch what is going on. I'll give them a quick "Hey buddy" glance to acknowledge them but I keep my attention to the hole. Most parents guard may be up a bit (understandably) with their kids talking to a stranger. I make it pretty clear that I am focused on my detecting. Usually watch for a few seconds and then ask "what 'cha doing?" Or "what are you looking for?".

I'll explain I am looking for lost coins that people have dropped. Often times by this point the parent has sauntered over so I'll talk with them too. If I get a strong signal I'll show how the pinpointer shows where it is and then I'll dig it for them.

I like to mention that although really old stuff is more rare, we do a lot of cleaning up as we go along. Its a good chance to show off the inevitable pull tabs and bottle caps I've been recovering from underneath their feet.

I make a point of showing how we dig plugs and then refill our holes every time. "I try to make it so that no one can even tell I dug here once I am done".

When I talk to people about MDing I like for them to understand the good things that we do. Cleaning up the area is a big part of that.

Here is an example conversation that can create leads for you:

Adult: "Have any luck?"

Me: "Its such a great day to be here at the park (beach etc). Nothing much found yet today but I wish their was a bounty on aluminum can pull tabs! While the park (beach etc) can be fun I prefer to detect on older property. Anything built from 1950 or earlier. Usually places with barns or a field on the property are what really get me excited. It is pretty cool what old relics can be found on most older properties"

Them: "Hmm… well I (my father, my neighbor etc) have a couple of acres that has been around for about 100 years. It does have a small field and a barn. Is that something you would be up for detecting?"

Me: "Wow! Yes, that sounds great. My name is Tim by the way…" and we start working out the details.

So the main take away from this one is talk to

everyone you get an opportunity to. Especially if they express even a bit of interest in what you are doing.

Show them how its done. Let them see how you are responsible and won't damage their property. Let them give it a try. Perhaps show them a couple of small items you have collected.

I intentionally keep a few old silver coins with me in an altoid tin filled with cotton. I explain that my son and I have a small coin collection and we are trying to collect every year of coins.

I DON'T show off rings or jewelry or else this sets up the wrong mental picture. Now they might be envisioning you coming and taking valuables off their property. Instead let them see it is an innocent and fun hobby that they could try as well.

Once you get used to this type of dialog it becomes second nature. You'll actually start looking forward to strangers showing interest in what you are doing while you are out detecting.

Use these new found skills to mention your hobby where ever you go. Whether its getting your hair cut, out golfing, at your kid's baseball games… you get the point. Spread the word and once someone understands what it is you do and are looking for, you will be amazed at the opportunities that open up. Understand that one connection can often lead to others. Direct referrals from someone's friend are rarely turned down.

Super User Tip: With social media it is now even easier than ever.

Here is the exact word for word post I made on Facebook to my local friends:

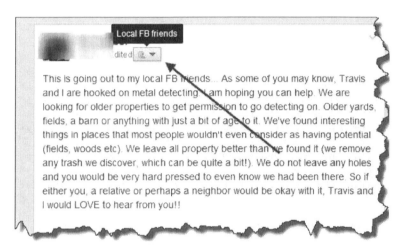

Notice the red arrow. When you post you can choose who gets to see your posting. In my case, I selected "Local FB Friends". Facebook knows who is local to you (within an hour or two drive) and will only post it on their walls. I didn't want to bother having friends in other countries seeing the post as it was not relevant to what I was looking for.

With in minutes I received 3 solid leads from my

friends. Here's some example replies back:

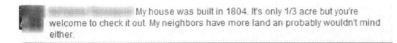

My house was built in 1804. It's only 1/3 acre but you're welcome to check it out. My neighbors have more land an probably wouldn't mind either.

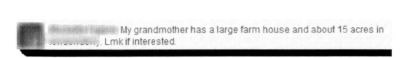

My grandmother has a large farm house and about 15 acres in . Lmk if interested.

All of these were solid leads.

I plan on doing a posting such as that about once a year or so. I'll thank the ones from last time and then restate the request for new leads.

This is a proven strategy for nice, new locations.

Using Google Earth

Before going out to a new spot to metal detect, I like to check out the spot "now and then" in time. That is, take a look of what may have changed in that location over time. Often times it can be quite informative. I have totally redirected my tactics many times based on what this 2 minutes of research has revealed to me time and again.

I use the free Google Earth program to do this.

Google Earth is a very close cousin to Google Maps but they are not the same.

If you've ever used Google Maps then Google Earth will be nearly as easy. You will need the stand alone version of Google Earth, not a version which comes as a plug in to Google Maps.

You can download it free here:
http://www.google.com/earth/explore/products/desktop.html

Once you install it type in the address of where you are about to go detecting. Then zoom in tight enough to see the area in good detail.

If you have a mouse with a wheel on it, turning the wheel forward zooms in and vice versa. You can also use the + plus and - minus keys on your keyboard for that as well.

Once I have located my target spot, I click on the clock icon in the top of the Google Earth program. I have a red arrow pointing to it below.

Then using the slider (shown with the yellow arrow) I can slide between now and decades ago. Older photos don't tend to have the same resolution but you can still make out details.

Here is an example of a park as seen from a recent satellite photo. (If you are viewing this in an ebook you should be able to double tap or pinch and zoom to see a larger version of this picture):

Now by sliding the time bar to 1992, I am taken more than 20 years back in time as shown here:

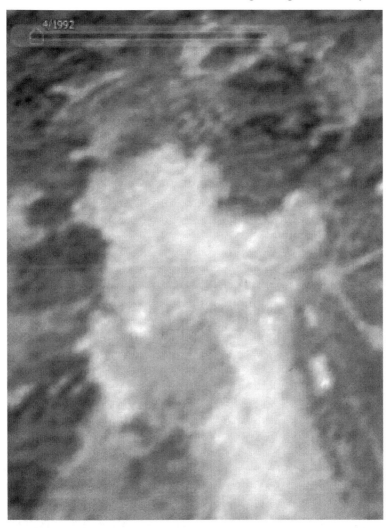

The interesting thing for me is that the park had changed orientation. The ball field was moved over from where it used to exist. Information such as this may help you decide to focus on a different area a bit.

In this example, I decided to make sure I hit the left

side of the picture more so than I would have. These days the left side is the outfield of the new baseball field. Not a particularly interesting spot except when I realize that it didn't always used to be the ball field. Instead in 1992 it was the majority of open space in the field. In other words prior to changing it probably had quite a bit more activity than it does now.

Now I do NOT advocate going out and digging up a ball field. Especially during a game. It tends to upset the umpires (kidding). I did however focus more on the tree line / outfield area and was rewarded for my efforts with some coins from the 1800's. I never would have bothered with that spot without this knowledge.

Google Earth is such a great research tool, I should do a book just on using it to its fullest!

Looking down you can identify things which are not immediately visible when you are on the ground.

Tip: I love looking for through each of the years which the satellite imagery is available in it. Photos taken during the winter or early spring are the best views. While the plants are still bare, details really pop out. The difference between looking at a wooded location in the spring versus summer is night and day.

Do yourself a favor and play around with Google Earth a bit. You will be glad you did. It is amazing what information you can gain about your next upcoming metal detecting hunt.

CHAPTER FIVE

Treasures Found: What Did I Just Dig Up?

Treasures Found: What Did I Just Dig Up?!?

So you've finally decided to hit an old yard or field to try you hand at relic hunting. Nice!

You get a solid hit on a target and uncover an amazing... hmm... ?

You will inevitably discover many "whatitz" items that look interesting if only could figure out what it actually was.

A great place to turn is some of the popular metal detecting forums. Many have sub forums just for the purpose of identifying something. Odds are you haven't found a one of a kind piece of metal. Most likely somebody, somewhere in this world has an idea of what it is.

Here is one good forum to try. It is the "What is it?" sub forum at Treasurenet.com

http://www.treasurenet.com/forums/what/

Simply post a picture and in a matter of hours your mystery may be solved.

A friendly reminder. Until you know what something

is and whether it is valuable, it is a good idea not to clean it. You could devalue something to nearly worthless so wait before proceeding.

If you want to try your hand at identifying something take a look. The last time I looked they had well over 32,000 (!) items posted there.

It is Jewelry, But Is It Real?

I won't lie. Its pretty exciting looking down in your scoop or in the hole to find a nice looking ring looking back at you.

Besides looking nice, with the price of gold these days a real gold ring has some legitimate value.

Before you get TOO excited, be sure to check out what type of metal it is made of.

Thankfully the far majority of legitimate jewelry pieces these days have markings on them indicating what type of metal is used. In rings you will find it inside the band of the ring.

Pure gold is 24K. That is not something you are likely to see on jewelry very often however because that is soft and easily scratched. 24K gold may look different than the usual gold you see in that it has a deeper yellow/orange tone to it.

Most jewelry instead is mixed with other metals to toughen it up for durability purposes. Depending on what it is mixed with, it often affects the color of the gold. It may become more pale for example.

The closer the K number is to 24K the higher the percentage of gold it has. K is short for Karat (total weight in gold). This is not to be confused with Carat which is what diamonds are measured by.

Normally you will see the K number but occasionally there will be a 3 digit number signifying what percent of pure gold it is.

The easy to remember formula to figure out how much pure gold is in an item is to take the K number and divide it by 24.

So for example a 14K ring. 14 divided by 24 = .583

14K (or 583) is 58.3% pure gold.

This is used in 90% of wedding bands by the way due to its durability. Since it is going to be used everyday on someone's hand, quite often they opt for 14K.

18K (or 750) is 75% pure gold. This is the most common purity of gold used for jewelry in Europe and Asia.

10K is 42%.

22K is 92% pure.

It should be obvious but... the higher the purity of gold, the more expensive it is.

If you had 18K ring and wanted to know what its melt value is you can do quick math for a ball park estimate. If gold was at $1,300 an ounce and you had a 1 ounce, 18K ring then the full gold value would be: 1300.00 x .75 = $975

If you sent that ring to a refinery (like www.midwestrefineries.com) they would give you 95% of the gold value for it. So within a week of sending it out, you would get a check for around $925. Congrats! You just paid for all of your metal detecting gear. Looks like its time to upgrade. Kidding. Well, maybe.

Returning Jewelry

You may occasionally find some jewelry that has clues as to who the owner is. In particular it is not uncommon for rings to be inscribed with their owners initials. School rings with the class year and the initials inscribed are quite often able to be returned to the rightful owner. To me it seems the morally right thing to at least try but that is up to you. I think you will be rewarded in karma points if you do return it.

If it is a cool enough story you may want to get the local newspaper involved. They love the "lost and returned" aspects of stories like that.

In the story it may be worth mentioning that you are willing to help out others if they lost something. Also that you are looking for older property to metal detect on. You never know, the act of returning that jewelry may lead to some of your best digs ever. Karma has a way of being good to good people!

Caring for and Cleaning Your Coins

You are going to find plenty of coins while metal detecting. Some of them may be quite old. You will want to protect your finds from the moment you discover them.

If you are not careful, considerable damage can be done to a coin with your digging tools. A nick or scrape on a rare coin would be pretty heartbreaking.

When it comes to coins, there are 3 different values:

Face Value - that is a quarter that is nothing special is worth a quarter.

Metal value - a beat up gold coin which may not have any collectors value still has valuable metal in it. There are refineries that could melt it down and pay you for its gold (or silver) content.

Numismatic Value - this is what a rare coin may be worth to coin collectors. Sometimes small differences in coins mean a lot to a coin collector so it may not be immediately obvious if you have something of value unless it is obviously very old. A rare mint mark or a very obscure mint defect can dramatically escalate a coin's value.

When deciding whether to clean a coin don't do it for any that you have a strong suspicion that it may be valuable to a collector.

Don't even rub it.

Some older coins can be quite soft.

Silica is one of the hardest substances on earth. It is found in sand and sandpaper. The simple act of rubbing dirt or sand off a coin can easily put scratches across the face of the coin. Coins are graded by condition and you could turn a quite valuable find into something considerably less valuable by cleaning it. Don't worry. That point is so important it will be repeated.

If you can't help yourself, LIGHTLY dust it off or blow on it until you get home. Some people keep a soft lens brush with them. These are the type of brushes used to clean camera lenses so they are very gentle.

Just don't rub it between your fingers. You might as well be rubbing sand paper across it. Of course if you are already sure it has no numismatic value then you don't need to be quite as cautious.

Note: If you strongly suspect that the coin could be very valuable, don't do ANYTHING to it. Don't even clean it with water. Protect it from any further damage and get it professionally looked at. Collectors often want it in "just found" condition without any tarnish or patina rubbed off it. Once they buy a coin they may decide to clean it with their methods but you should leave that choice to them. Once they have paid you the big bucks they can do what ever they want to it.

If you have determined that the coin has no coin collector value then you can clean them when you get home. Sponges which have a plastic scrubbing surface don't tend to damage coins but it's always smart to test first.

Its a good idea to keep a collection of "junk" or face value coins in uncleaned condition. You can then experiment with them one at a time using various cleaning methods to judge the results. This will give you an idea of the expected results if you do use that cleaning method "for real".

An important point to remember is that different coins react differently to different cleaning methods. What may work like a charm on your old nickel may irreparably ruin your silver. That's why you want to proceed slowly and test on some least desirable coins first.

Cleaning Silver Coins

Silver coins are soft. As mentioned, dirt is abrasive and hard. Do not rub dirt off silver coins. You will be tempted (believe me) but wait until you get home. When (not if) you can't help yourself and you DO rub it, you will be create micro scratches across on the silver, so do wait if you can stand it. It may not be a big deal on a mercury dime or a common date silver but if its a rarer minted or desirable coin, you could be cutting its value down significantly with one rub.

When you get home let it sit in water for several minutes to help loosen up any dirt. Then rinse it under running water. Often that is all you will need to do.

If the coin has no collector value and it still has dirt, take a soft toothbrush. While it is still under the running water, dab the toothbrush up and down. You can also take a Q tip and (again under running water) dab it up and down to get the rest of the dirt. Take your time and it will be cleaned off without scratches.

Silver often cleans off beautifully pretty easily.

Least Intrusive Method

There are many (many) suggestions on using various ingredients on coins. Most variations of these can be found on Youtube.

Keep mind that they are usually are either caustic (acidic) or abrasive. That means by nature they all stand a chance of damaging a coin. If you use the wrong substance or forget to neutralize it when you are done, it can continue to eat away at the coin. You may find that you just "toasted" your coin. I personally have erased dates off of some coins by either rubbing too hard or testing new recipes. It is bound to happen so give it some trial and error on normal coins first. Do that before you ever think of doing it to an older coin in your collection. An older coin you don't plan on selling that is!

I'll start with what I think is one of the better methods to try (and a non-valuable coin!!!). It does involve a bit of labor but if you find a cool coin you want to add to your display collection, this one can likely help with that. Its best to watch the video on it so you can see the technique first hand. The link is here:

https://www.youtube.com/watch?v=cGZ9yYD6i6k

Quick Cleaning Non-valuable Coins

One of the quickest way to get direct and light debris off a coin is using baking soda. Note I said baking soda not baking powder. For all you non-cooks out there, those are two different things.

I lightly put about 1/2 a teaspoon full in a small bowl. Add just the littlest bit of water. Enough to get it damp to form a paste. Then I pinch a bit of it with my forefinger and thumb. Next I pick up a damp coin and start gently rubbing it. You are likely to start seeing the baking soda start to turn black as it removes the dirt.

Baking soda is a key ingredient in toothpaste by the way. It is what gives the toothpaste a bit of abrasive grit to help clean your teeth. Because of this, I have also used some Colgate tooth paste successfully as well on old (non valuable!) coins. Use the same procedure as outlined above to run the toothpaste onto the coin.

Quick Cleaning Large Quantities of Clad Coins

To clean a bunch of coins on a budget, grab a small quart container. Like those used for milk or orange juice. Thoroughly clean it out first. Then put in an inch or two of sand. Pour in 1/2 a cup of vinegar and 1/2 a cup of water. Put the cover on and start shaking!

After a good work out you can strain the coins out and rinse them well to get the vinegar off. Remember this is for non-valuable clad coins old. Anything cleaned with this process will be worthless to a coin collector for numismatic value. I have mason jars filled with my old clad. I can periodically take those to a "Coinstar" machine at a local grocery store. I pour the coins into it, it spits out any bad ones and then pays me for them. They take a generous fee (7% I believe) but its a quick way to cash them in.

What is it Worth?

You have found what appears to be a really old coin or button. In doing your research it looks like it would have some value to a collector.

The million dollar question is: what is it worth?

The answer is simple. Its worth what ever the market is willing to pay for it.

Assuming you don't have a one of a kind item, the odds are very good that someone has sold similar items to yours in the past. The first stop to start researching its value should be Ebay (www.ebay.com).

Let's say you dug up a very desirable George Washington (GW) Inaugural Button. Any legitimate George Washington era item is desired by quite a few collectors.

Here is how to find out how much they have been going for lately.

1) Go to www.ebay.com

2) Up top, near the search bar, click on the "Advanced" link to the top right

This brings up the advanced search page. Fill it out as

shown below:

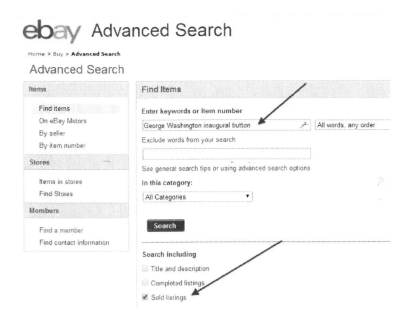

Then scroll down a bit for this:

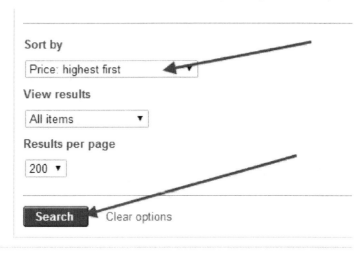

Remember you can either pinch to zoom in on those images or double tap them.

Either way, they are showing to choose the "Sold Listings" box as well as "Sort by Price: highest first".

You will see recent sold listings for the item. Here is an example.

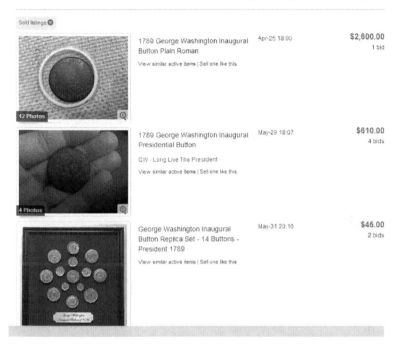

Sold listings

	1789 George Washington Inaugural Button Plain Roman	Apr-25 18:00	$2,600.00 1 bid
	View similar active items | Sell one like this		
	1789 George Washington Inaugural Presidential Button	May-29 18:07	$610.00 4 bids
	GW - Long Live The President		
	View similar active items | Sell one like this		
	George Washington Inaugural Button Replica Set - 14 Buttons - President 1789	May-31 20:10	$45.00 2 bids
	View similar active items | Sell one like this		

The image above has prices wildly varying from $2,600, $610 and $45

Looking at each description and their pictures will help you understand why the price variations.

The first one is a GW button in very good condition with sharp details. That sold for $2,600

The second is a barely readable GW button but it still managed to get $610

The last one is a collection of replica buttons so that doesn't apply. It does bring up the fact that you want to make sure that your item is legitimate and not replica or fake. To help determine that, its not a bad idea to post VERY clear and close up photos on some of the more popular treasure hunting forums (like treasurenet.com or metaldetectingforum.com). Ask for people's thoughts. If there is anything misleading about your find, someone is very likely to help point it out to you. You may even get some messages offering to buy it if it looks good.

Getting it Appraised

If you are pretty sure that the year or mint mark from your coin make it collectible, then it may be worth have a Numismatic appraiser take a look at it. They can also grade the condition of it. Have a grading can help you when you go to sell it, particularly it is in a high grading level.

Avoid the Pawnshop

That title says it all. Unless you want to get bottom dollar for your find then you are usually better off selling it away from a pawn shop. If you need cash instantly to bail out your favorite uncle and you don't care about getting top dollar… then perhaps you can consider it. They are the business of making money and that doesn't happen by paying top dollar. Despite what the guys on "Pawn Star" may portray.

Melt Value of Precious Metal

If you decide you don't want to sell an item on ebay
you can consider melting it down for its metal value.
Particularly gold or platinum. It always fetches a
premium.

You can quickly figure out what the metal value of an
item is but it does require you to be able to preciously
weight it.

Here is an example of an inexpensive, precise digital
scale which can weight your jewelry:
http://amzn.to/1mabkkS

Once you have the weight, head over to this this
precious metal value calculator:

http://dendritics.com/metal-calc/

Here is an example screen shot of it. As an example if
you found an 18K yellow gold ring that weighted 8
grams. It calculates the value of it based on that days
price for that precious metal. Besides gold, you can
also choose silver, platinum or palladium.

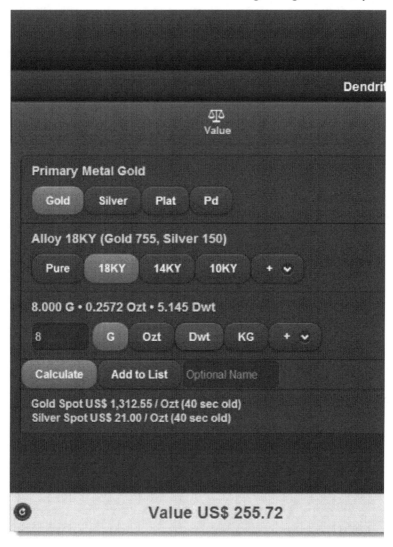

At the bottom you will see the melt value for that

amount of metal.

Now how to get the money from it?

One avenue that people use is to send it to a refinery. One that is used by quite a few people I know is Mid West Refineries:
http://www.midwestrefineries.com/

In the case of Mid West refineries, the payout for gold is 95%. In this case, the $255.72 calculated above would result in a check of about $242 from them.

I would recommend sending one item in to test how comfortable you are with the process. They weigh it and will send you a check for the amount within a couple of days. Then you can send more items in quantities that you are comfortable with.

This is a FAR better return than a pawnshop or "Cash for Gold!" business will give you.

...Or You Can Keep It

You will likely be amazed how many detectorists don't sell most (or any) of their finds. They seem to get more satisfaction out of building a huge collection of found items.

Considering the precious nature of the items, its not a

bad little back up plan if the economy takes a really, really bad turn for the worse. I can think of worse things than having a collection of gold, platinum and silver when times are tough.

Tracking Your Progress

Someone moving beyond the beginner's stage for metal detecting may start wishing to log in their detecting activity.

I have a simple but effective Google spreadsheet doc that I use.

Here is a look at it in 2 separate images due to the width the spreadsheet:

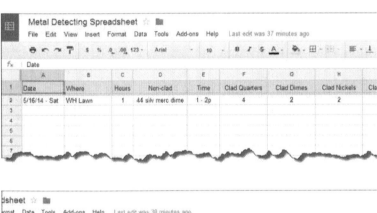

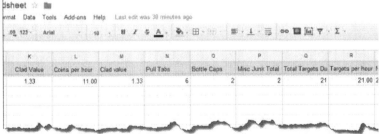

I have it set to calculate a few things every time I make an entry. It calculates:

* The value of that day's clad coins
* The total number of targets (including junk) dug up that day
* How many targets I dug up per hour (including junk targets)
* The GPS coordinates of exactly where the hunt was

For the GPS coordinates, I simply go to http://maps.google.com

Then I find the location and zoom in. Once I see the spot, I left click my mouse. In the upper left corner of the screen, it shows me the GPS coordinates of that location which I copy and paste into the spreadsheet.

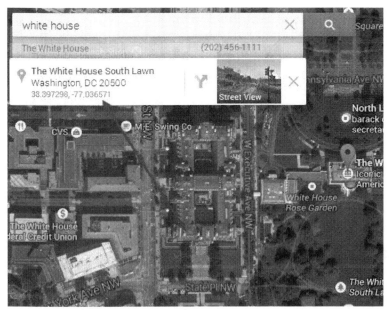

I don't put in GPS for every hunt. Only for new hunt locations as I go along. It is great for reference in the future if I am a bit unclear or want to give those to a hunting buddy to meet there.

You may not understand why you would want to keep a spreadsheet until you have a few dozen hunts under your belt. It is very helpful to look back and analyze the "hot spots" with the most targets, oldest targets etc.

I also make dated entries as to when I change the batteries in my detector and Pro Pointer. I know that I average about 22 hours on 4 AA Duracell batteries with my Garrett detector for example. This can give me an idea of when I will be running out in the future.

You can also see improvements over time.

I make notes of when I get better equipment as well. Whether it be a new pinpointer tool, digging tool or scoop.

As an example I recently upgraded my water scoop and found that I am digging up a bit more than 3 times as many targets now because the scoop is such a big help. That helps me realize the value of investing in better equipment.

This helps to give you a broader perspective over time as far as what activity (and where) is yielding the results that you are most interested in going after.

I would gladly share this spreadsheet with any friend that wanted it. To save you from asking, here you go:

http://bit.ly/WaTr0a

Feel free to copy that and modify it in any way that you want for your own uses. One suggestion is to add a column for rings for example if you want to track that.

I highly recommend tracking it your progress!

Photographing Your Finds

As you dig up some interesting finds, you may want to start taking snapshots to remember them by. If you decide to sell (or give away) some of your items, its nice to have a memento of what you had unearthed. A more common reason to want to photograph will likely be to share it on one of the many metal detecting forums. It is an accomplishment to get something cool and MDers are very supportive of each others finds.

I decided to add this chapter after some successful water hunting recently. I had shown this photo in a previous chapter on fresh water hunting. It was my finds in a recent 2 week period.

That photograph looks pretty good (if I do say so myself!). It was very easy to get.

First, take a look at the photo as it actually first appeared here:

Here are my tips on getting it to look so good:

* Place the items on a white background. I used a notebook which happened to be lying near by.

* Position the items in a way that is a bit interesting visually and also shows off the best angles of the items. The one thing I should have done in these pictures is to show the jewelers marks in the bands if

possible. For example if the ring has 18K or 925 (sterling silver) then its good to try and include that as well for future reference.

* Use natural light. I put these on a bed which had sunlight coming in. It was a bit overcast which is actually perfect as it filters the sun a bit. A sunny day may have over lit the items a bit.

* After taking the photo use the crop tool to cut out all unwanted background.

* Be sure you save the images fairly large so you can see detail. Most smart phones these days automatically save images at very high resolution. Just make sure you aren't killing the detail by saving it at small resolution or using too much image compression.

I took this on my Samsung Galaxy S4 phone. It includes a crop option as do most smart phones these days.

I think looking at the before and after photos, you will agree these simple steps make a big difference.

Its a great way to capture a good round of metal detecting.

By the way, in that photo the chain at the bottom is 14K gold. Its melt down value in gold alone was about

$170 when it was found. Mailing that out to a refinery such as MidWest Refineries would result in a check for 95% of that value being mailed back to me. How many hobbies do you know of that you can do that?

CHAPTER SIX

Appendices

Appendix A: Brief History of Detecting

I saved this for towards the end of the book. Its not essential knowledge for you to enjoy your hobby but being the geek that I am, I think its pretty cool.

Trivia question: any idea who invented the first metal detector?

Spoiler alert. The answer is on the next line. Did you guess yet?

Alexander Graham Bell. He created it out of necessity. In 1881 President James Garfield lay dying from an assassin's bullet. The doctors could not locate it in his body. Being the smart guy that he was, within hours he came up with an electro magnetic detecting device that he called the induction balance machine. It was a large apparatus and not particular mobile.

It was actually working. Sort of. The problem is, the President was on a coil spring bed (made of metal) so it was throwing the results off.

Unfortunately it didn't work as well as hoped and the President died.

Fast forward to 1925.

Gerhard Fisher is credited with invented one of the first hand held metal detector.

The ironic thing is he did not set out to make a metal detector. Instead his job at the time was to create "airborne direction finding equipment". In doing his research he discovered some strange errors and issues concerning radio waves and metal. He turned that knowledge into the first truly practical metal detectors.

In 1931 he created the first commercially selling models and it was a large scale production. Fisher detectors are still sold to this day.

Side note: history purists may argue that another gentleman at the time, Shirl Herr, actually beat him to the patent office by a few months. Unfortunately for Herr, Fisher's patent was approved first.

Advancements in the Technology

Nothing spurs creativity like war and WWII was no exception. The Polish Army took Herr's version of detector and modified it heavily. They created a big, bulky but effective machine used extensively against the German's. It was used to find land mines that they buried everywhere. It worked so great that they ordered 500 of them for their army.

After the war, other refinements to the technology kept emerging. One for example was Charles Garrett's "Beat Frequency Oscillator" (BFO). Garrett is still around today and is the maker of a model that I recommend for people starting out.

If that hasn't quenched your geek appetite for metal detecting history, you can read quite a bit more here: http://en.wikipedia.org/wiki/Metal_detector

Appendix B: Online Resources

Here are some of my favorite bookmarked resources. These are handy when you are online. If you wish to have an email sent to you with all of links in this book, please email me at tim@metaldetectortips.com. For a subject in that email please use: "Metal Detecting Links" and I will send them to you free of charge.

If you have one that you absolutely LOVE and want to share, please let me know. You can email me at: tim@metaldetectortips.com

Forums

http://metaldetectingforum.com/
http://www.treasurenet.com/forums/metal-detecting-forum/
http://www.americandetectorist.com/forum/

Metal Detecting blogs:

http://www.stoutstandards.com/Coinhunting.html
http://www.mapsurfer.com/blog/ (incredible silver coin

detectorist!)
http://dirtgirlmetaldetecting.blogspot.com/
http://theringfinders.com/blog/

Metal Detecting Podcasts to Listen to:

http://danhughes.libsyn.com/category/treasure
http://www.letstalkmetaldetectingandtreasurehunting.com/blog/

Online Metal Detecting Newsletters:

The Garrett Searcher:
http://www.garrett.com/hobbysite/hbby_newsletter.aspx (Be sure to look through past editions by clicking the drop down box in the center of the screen)

Youtube

Some of my favorite metal detecting channels. Search Youtube.com for:
Nuggetnoggin
Beau Ouimette
Chicagoron
Malcolmpotter
JDsCoins
Stealthdiggers
CTTodd1

Clubs

List of Metal Detector Clubs in the U.S.
www.kellycodetectors.com/clubs/index.htm

Metal Detector Clubs around the world:
http://gometaldetecting.com/links-clubs.htm

Research

Building and Structure Research
Old buildings: http://www.farmbuildingguide.org
Old stone structures: http://www.stonestructures.org

Old Maps
http://www.historicmapworks.com/

Coin Research
http://www.coinflation.com
http://sammler.com/coins/coinvalues.htm
World Coins: http://worldcoingallery.com/
U.S. Older Coins:
http://www.collect1.coinsandstamps.com/

Colonial and Civil War Button Research
1)
http://www.historicalimagebank.com/gallery/main.php
2) Search for: button

3) Press the "show all button"

Some Places to Buy Detectors and Accessories
First, check to see if there are any shops local to you.
Most detector's prices are pretty standard among
dealers. If you can help support a local dealer, that is
the recommended route. You may actually end up
paying less especially if they are sponsoring one of the
many detecting blogs.

www.amazon.com
www.kellycodetectors.com
www.bigboyshobbies.net

Where to Sell Coins
www.ebay.com

Where to Sell Scrap Precious Metal
http://www.midwestrefineries.com

Old / Rare Book Finder
http://www.addall.com/Used/

Do you have a resource to share? Please do! You can
reach me at tim@metaldetectortips.com

Appendix C: Success Stories

I love reading about and/or watching Youtube videos of metal detecting success stories.

I thought I would share a few with you.

These are handy when you are at your computer. If you wish to have an email sent to you with all of links in this book, please email me at tim@metaldetectortips.com. For a subject in that email please use: "Metal Detecting Links" and I will send them to you free of charge.

If this doesn't get you motivated, I am not sure what will!

Its exciting finding an old coin. But how about a REALLY old coin. Like this one from the 1300's. This was found using a Garrett Euro Ace. That is the equivalent to the Ace 350 which is just one model up from my recommended starter machine the 250. They are both very similar except for coil size and some discrimination changes. Anyways, here is that coin find:
https://www.youtube.com/watch?v=QZAaCRJAqrk

A modern day cache with some nice coins in it. The videos a bit long but if you skip forward a bit, you will get the point!
https://www.youtube.com/watch?v=LkAs5UkQ8zA

This is a VERY nice find of **178 silver coins found in a stream**. He is using a Garrett AT Pro (All Terrain Pro) which is waterproof. I only mention that because, again it is waterproof. Some detectors (including the Ace 250) can get their coils wet but their control panel area is NOT water proof. Other machines are made for an environment such as the one in the video. It pays off nicely for him.
https://www.youtube.com/watch?v=JDC3SUK3axM

This same guy from the video above goes back to the same spot a year later and discovers more treasure there. The same warnings about using a waterproof detector apply. He uses a AT Pro which is waterproof.
https://www.youtube.com/watch?v=AiqNb_IHfo8

Parent's Buried Cache

Here's a fun one. The property owner knew that his wife's parents had caches buried on the property. Unfortunately they were long dead and the maps they had made references to landmarks which were no longer there. So they called in the specialists. Check out the very large detector they use for deep searches. They also used Garret AT Pro's in this recovery operation as well. Talk about large caches. How about wheel barrels full?
https://www.youtube.com/watch?v=Ctz_O-QrwJg

Want to see what it feels like to find real gold while

underwater detecting? This video is pretty cool. I am pretty sure the diver's hand is shaking once he realizes what he has found:
http://on.fb.me/PTibpM

Now for TRUE buried treasure, nothing beats a good "horde" finding. Here are 8 recent hordes of coins and jewels found just in England. Some are from the Romans who hid the stashes with plans of coming back to retrieve them. Some of these had over **50,000 ancient coins in one spot**. Imagine being one of the metal detector hobbyists who stumbled across these:
http://bit.ly/R6jvXg

Here is what it is like **finding gold nuggets**. It gives a good sense of how it is a bit different than normal detecting. They use a Garrett AT Gold detector in this video. (AT stands for All Terrain = waterproof):
https://www.youtube.com/watch?v=tkeWqZYE-HM

True Pirates Hoard

Many movies and books have plot lines about pirates burying a chest full of gold and silver. Sometimes they embellish things further by having a skeleton or two thrown in for good measure to liven up the story. Well this is a true story of exactly those circumstances.

Back in 1947, treasure hunter Edward Rowe Snow purchased what was reported to be a genuine pirate's map. It was supposedly created by pirate Edward Low in the 1800's. It took Snow about 5 years to get to the remote island off Nova Scotia that he believed the map was portraying. Armed with the map and his metal detector, he set off for Isle Haute. After much digging one day he was almost done for the night when his detector started giving off strange readings.

After about 20 minutes of digging, he found some human ribs in the dirt. A few more swings and his axe became stuck in something. That turned out to be a human skull which pulled out of the ground and rolled across his feet. He was understandably a bit spooked out as it was now getting dark. He arrived back first thing in the morning accompanied by some friends. They recovered Spanish and Portuguese gold coins that were over 200 years old.

There may be more still buried there but you'll probably never get the chance to find out. The Isle is now heavily protected and visitors are not welcome without a lot of government approval.

You can read a bit more about this find in this 1952 edition of Life Magazine:
Http://bit.ly/1szu0U7

Various detector manufacturers also ask for success stories from their users. Some are pretty cool to read through. They are average people finding some very interesting and sometimes valuable things.

Minelab success stories:
http://www.minelab.com/consumer/success-stories
Garrett Hall of Fame finds:
http://www.garrett.com/hobbysite/hall_of_fame_galler
y_003.aspx (be sure to click the Next page link at the
bottom of each page)
Kellyco success stories:
http://www.kellycodetectors.com/treasure-stories/

Do you have a favorite detecting success video to
share? If so, send me a link. I LOVE checking them
out. You can reach me at tim@metaldetectortips.com

Appendix D: Metal Detector Manuals

For your reference, I have compiled a list of the various owners manuals for some of most popular metal detecting machines.

This is by no means a comprehensive list of all the machines that are worthy of being owned. It is just some of the most popular makers in case you want to check out their manuals.

Bounty Hunter - All models:
http://www.detecting.com/manuals.htm
DX Deus -
http://www.xpmetaldetectors.com/images/update_deus
/User_manual_UK_V3.0_WEB.pdf
Fisher - All models:
http://www.fisherlab.com/hobby/manuals.htm
Garrett - All models:
http://www.garrett.com/hobbysite/hbby_manuals.aspx
Minelab - All models:
http://www.minelab.com/consumer/knowledge-
base/product-manuals
Teknetics - All models:
http://www.tekneticst2.com/manuals-specs.htm
Tesoro - All models:
http://www.tesoro.com/info/manuals/manuals.html
White's - All models:
http://www.whiteselectronics.com/support/manuals

Final Words

It is our sincere hope that you have picked up some great information in this ebook. We have made it as practical as possible and included a lot of information that I wish I knew when I first getting started.

If you have suggestions on how to make this book even better, I am all ears! I may add that information in and as a thank you I will send you an updated copy of the book, free of charge.

My son Travis and I are always looking for new and interesting places to detect. We are willing to travel to them. If you have an interesting hunt coming up and want some company, drop me an email! tim@metaldetectortips.com - I'm more than happy to have you check out any of our gear if you want.

Last but certainly not least… reviews of this ebook on Amazon are really important and sincerely appreciated. If you can take a moment and leave one, you have Travis' and my gratitude.

Thanks and happy hunting!

Tim and Travis

Dedication

This book is dedicated to our friend and mentor, Bill Myers.

Bill introduced both Travis and I to metal detecting and had us hooked within 30 seconds.

He was not only was gracious with his time but then said "hey guys, why don't you borrow my equipment for the next two days?". 2 days, 4 beaches and many hours together as father and son had us converted.

This photo captures our life changing moment. This is Bill Myers going over the basics with Travis and Julia at a beach in Florida. Little did we know!

Bill Myer's has an exceptional DVD on metal detecting here which is available at his website here: www.bmyers.com

Once again you have changed our lives for the better Bill and we thank you for that.

Made in the USA
Middletown, DE
17 October 2016